More of the Real Life...
FREDDIE MERCURY

HIS FRIENDS AND COLLEAGUES PAY TRIBUTE

More of the Real Life...

FREDDIE MERCURY

by
David Evans and David Minns

BRITANNIA PRESS PUBLISHING

Copyright © 1992 Britannia Press Publishing.

First edition *This is the Real Life...* published in Great Britain in 1992.
Second edition *This is the Real Life...* published in Great Britain in 1994.
Third edition *More of the Real Life...* published in Great Britain 1995.

British Library Cataloguing in Publication Data.
A Catalogue record for this book is available from the British Library.
        Evans, Minns
        More of the Real Life... Freddie Mercury

        ISBN 1-899784-20-9

Printed and bound in Great Britain by WBC, Bridgend.
Cover photograph: Rex Features Ltd.

Britannia Press Publishing is a division of Britannia Crest International Ltd.
72 Chalk Farm Road, London NW1 8AN.
2.10 The Schoolhouse, Pages Walk, London SE1 4HG.

*This book is dedicated to
Freddie's parents whom many of us never met.
We would like them to know how much their son was loved.*

This book is also dedicated to the memory of Douglas Chalmers who, like Freddie, died in 1991 - too early.

———————◆●◆◆———————

I was Douglas' coexecutor and on removing the last of his possessions from his flat after its sale, I went into the kitchen to find that the new occupants had been in and cleared out what little had been left in drawers and cupboards for which they had no use.

Amongst some old telephone directories, a mug, a bent spoon and screwed-up bits of paper was a heart. Perhaps somewhat mawk-ish really, it was a stuffed, faded thing, originally made of red, glazed cotton, set with pins and patterns of twisted wool which someone had made after the First World War to hang on a wall to commemo-rate a loved one.

Pinned to it, an integral part of the design, was a woven label, the sort we used to wear in our games clothes at school. They must have been sold by the hundred thousand.

When the golden sun is sinking
And your mind from care set free
Whilst of others you are thinking
Will you sometimes think of me?

It seemed rather apt.

REMEMBER THE NAMES

David Evans

Contents

Other than reprints, this is the first opportunity we have had to include two very important tributes to Freddie which were not available in time for the first edition, those of James Arthurs and Peter Freestone. James was a great friend of Freddie's and Peter worked for *Queen* from 1979 and was, particularly, Freddie's P.A. for almost ten years. His knowledge of and regard for Freddie are both profound and so we take this opportunity to include some of the recollections of the man he worked for in health and tended to in illness.

We have included an epilogue which has turned out to be a roundup of some of the events and nonevents marking the aftermath of Freddie's death. We hope you find it illuminating and trust that further bulletins will be forthcoming as we progress to another edition. It seems there will always be something to add to the life of Freddie Mercury.

INTRODUCTION

Fame, celebrity, stardom... Wealth, success, renown... Curtain calls, applause, plaudits... Praise, eulogies, superlatives... He may have made a few mistakes but he was a star right to the end and Freddie loved being a star. He'd never wanted to be anything else.

I first met him in 1975 when, after three albums, the name of *Queen* was already being noised abroad. Freddie was known but he wasn't a star. After *Bohemian Rhapsody*, I watched him become a star; I watched him achieving his ambitions. He himself said on camera that he couldn't cook and that he was a "useless housewife" and so Freddie plumped for being a star. The reason that we aren't all stars is very simply that it's very difficult. You have to be fearless, seriously talented, a political genius on a par with Machiavelli, a crystal clear communicator and blessed with the stubbornness and perseverance of Hercules shovelling shit in the stables. I'm a much better cook than I would have been a star and so I and all his other friends and confidantes were quite happy to get on with our lives as he got on with his, but always frequently touching base over the years to reaffirm where we had come from, who we were, how far we'd come and where we were going.

Latterly, Freddie knew only too well where he was going and he told me he wasn't afraid of that either.

So now he's gone... It's hard to believe but we have to believe it as we are left behind without him and we shall never be touched by stardom like his again. His had a frightening and unique logic about it which you might have seen had you known him for so long as we did. He achieved just about everything he wanted and above all he went out on top of his world, not sinking, not sliding, not skidding and slithering but fixed firmly on top, exactly where he put himself and it is inconceivable to think of him as being anywhere else. His star will never become tawdry or tarnished or slurred by failure and odious comparison. It will always shine as brightly as he left it. But we who are left behind have, nevertheless, lost our friend and I try to comfort myself by telling myself that I could not have imagined him as a sixty year old.

But on the other side of the coin, Freddie Mercury was a mortal man and it is strange to reflect that it was his very mortality which will probably render him immortal as myth becomes legend. That cold, conscience-less, random, wriggling virus, whilst contributing to his earthly demise, also insured his niche in eternity. Do you think if it knew, though, what it had done, that it would stop, recoiling in horror at its clinical thoroughness, as it watched us grieving over yet another one of its victims?

Of course, Freddie hated being ill and wanted no one to know, even his closest friends, until it was impossible for us not to guess what ailed him. This period of his life must have been really tough for him, this maintenance of Freddie Mercury, star, for he was an incredibly, often forcefully honest and open man and he hated having to hide. His admission to James Johnson in an interview in 1975 that he slept with both men and women pulled the rug out from silly, vicious speculation for a good number of years and allowed him to live a public private life which, although a teensy bit frantic for a while, was only so because he'd been a bit late starting. Privately, his life was as normal as he could have wanted it to be in the circumstances and, I'm glad to say, the late starter soon caught up.

His own life touched millions of others, most of whom had to be content to love him, nay adore him, from afar. For those of you like me who will always love and adore the boy and who have gone out and bought *Those Were The Days Of Our Lives*, when you look at the accompanying video, close your eyes and pretend you're there on the sound stage, watching the filming. At the end of each of the many takes during that day's shooting, open your eyes and you would have seen Freddie, crippled by an agonising condition which affected his foot, hobbling in great pain to his chair not to give up and go home, not to shrug and surrender and compromise with a merely so-so performance but to do it again and again and again until his perfectionism was satisfied.

That's a brave man and that's a star and that was my friend, for the best bit about being a star, the bit even stars don't know about and can't even begin to calculate, is that stars are only stars if they inspire and continue to inspire. Freddie inspired not only as a writer and as a musician and as a performer but ultimately as a man.

David Evans, November 1991

CONTRIBUTORS

David Evans
After University worked for Silvio Narizzano, the TV and film director before joining Barry Krost's office. General manager of John Reid Enterprises in *Queen* days. Left the music business to pursue a writing career. David is also the author of: *Cat Stevens* - The Boy Who Looked at the Moon; *Dusty Springfield* - Scissors and Paste; *From Mae to Madonna* - Glamour Blondes.

David Minns
Worked in costume and wardrobe for several years before joining Roger Clifford and Peter Thomson in Theatrical Publicity. Spent time at McCartney Productions before starting off his own artists' management company. Worked with Freddie in Freddie's Goose Productions Company before leaving to pursue a career in music publishing. Lately General Manager at Warner Chappell and currently working on both publishing and television production projects as well as a continuing interest in the management of several performing artists and songwriters.

Derrick Branche
Actor. Contemporary of Freddie's at school in India 1957-1962.

Eddie Howell
British with a dash of Viking. Songwriter, singer. Worked with Freddie in 1976 on single *Man From Manhattan* whilst managed by David Minns. Signed as recording artist to Warner BrothersRecords 1975 - 1978. Songs published by Chrysalis.

Peter Straker
Born in Jamaica, Peter arrived in England with his grandmother and brothers to join his mother and complete his schooling here before joining the company of *Hair* at the Shaftesbury Theatre where he played *Hud* for eighteen months before taking the part and the production to Norway. Has recorded many albums as well as pursuing a successful career as stage, television and film actor. Worked with Freddie on three albums. Currently back at the Shaftesbury Theatre as *The Phantom* in Ken Hill's original production of *Phantom of the Opera*.

Caroline Boucher
Music journalist writing for *Disc*. Press and Publicity Officer for John Reid Enterprises 1974-77, *Queens* management 1975 onwards. Handled all press and PR for *A Night At The Opera* and subsequent albums while the band was managed by John Reid.

Annie Nightingale
BBC Radio Disc Jockey and presenter. Well known for her personal tastes in music and great integrity. First woman DJ of consequence to present contemporary music in a serious and considered fashion. Co-presented *Old Grey Whistle Test* 1978 onwards.

Nina Myskow
Journalist and broadcaster. Editor *Jackie Magazine*, rock writer on *The Sun*, TV Critic *News of the World*, currently woman columnist in *The Sun*. Television appearances include *New Faces* and own shows on BSB. Prefers to be known as an ageing bimbette and apprentice bag lady.

Mike Moran
Composer, musician, musical director, record producer and arranger. Worked with Freddie on *The Great Pretender* single and the *Barcelona* album.

Jacky Gunn
Started work for *Queen* Productions in 1982 and has been there ever since. Her special responsibility is the fan club, some twenty thousand members spread over every country in the world.

Jim Jenkins
Works for the Port of Liverpool Authority. *Queen's* longest serving fan. Joined the fan club in February 1974 when it was run by Pat and Sue Johnson from Trident. Known as *The Queen Encyclopaedia* for which he gets teased unmercifully.

Paul Gambaccini
Journalist, broadcaster, writer, soft-ball player. Possessor of one of the finest integrities in the music business and one of the deepest and wide-ranging banks of knowledge and information about popular music.

Gordon Atkinson
Freddie's doctor, his GP since 1976. A good friend, confidante.

David Munns
Joined EMI records in the early seventies as general manager of the Label. Later MD of Polydor Records and now Senior Vice-President Pop Marketing at Polygram International.

Peter Hince
Freddie's personal roadie from 1975 until 1986. Previously worked for *Mott the Hoople* amongst others. Now a successful advertising photographer dealing with both fashion and people. Works out of own studio in the City and also on location.

Gary Langan
Record producer, owns highly successful Metropolis studio complex. One time tape operator/assistant at Sarm East, 1974 onwards. Worked with *Queen* on *Sheer Heart Attack, A Night At The Opera, A Day At The Races* and *News of the World.*

Chris Taylor
aka Crystal. Roger Taylor's roadie from 1975 onwards. Intimate of *Queen* and Freddie's.

Billy Squier
Born Boston. Now lives in New York. American songwriter and performer. Knew Freddie for many years and worked closely with him in the 1980s.

Tony Hadley
Lead singer with *Spandau Ballet.* Now also pursuing solo album and singles career.

Tim Rice
English writer and lyricist. Renowned for *Jesus Christ Superstar* and *Evita* amongst many other successes.

Ann Ortman
International jewellery designer and watercolour artist. Painted portraits of Freddie's cats in 1988.

Diana Moseley
Costume designer. Worked on several of Freddie's and *Queen's* videos and costumed the European *Magic* Tour in 1986.

Trevor Clarke
Friend and confidante. Always wanted to be an actor but found a better stage on which to entertain in the world of catering and nightclubs where he confesses to thinking of every night as a first night, a night to be remembered by people whom he wants to make happy.

Sarah Standing
As Sarah Forbes, daughter of film director Bryan and actress Nanette Newman, she worked for John Reid Enterprises 1976-1977 and was engaged to John Reid, *Queen*'s manager at the time.

Sarah Harrison
Has worked all her life in either fashion or entertainment. Associated with Browns of South Molton Street and later with Ralph Lauren. It was as Harvey Goldsmith's assistant for many years that she knew Freddie both personally and professionally. Now lives in France.

Nigel Quiney
Born Dulwich, London. Businessman and designer of gift wraps and greetings cards since the early sixties.

Cherry Brown
Ran Country Cousin cabaret restaurant and bar for many years. Early confidante of Freddie's. Now lives in Brighton, a tireless volunteer for Aids charities.

Elaine Paige
Star of countless West End musicals including *Evita*, and successful recording artist. Worked closely with Freddie when she recorded her *Queen Album*.

James Arthurs
Friend and confidante of Freddie.

Peter Freestone
Peter began his career at the Royal Opera House before working for *Queen* in charge of tour costumes. He became Freddie's P.A. in 1982 and remained with him until the end. He is now following a career in nursing but is keeping his hand in with the rock music business as a consultant to *The Fuse*, a six piece band from the Bournemouth area. His overview of the potential pitfalls as well as the keener strategies of the music business will be invaluable to the band and we wish them well. Peter is also still just as keen on opera and is deeply involved with the European Chamber Opera company.

I see a little silhouetto of a man

PART I

FIRST IMPRESSIONS

DERRICK BRANCHE

Thirty five years ago, in 1957, on a slow train winding it's way up to Poona in the hills from Bombay on the plains, the lives of five ten year old boys were quite arbitrarily thrown together as they mingled, all strangers, with the remainder of the train's passengers who would all have been en route to their respective boarding schools in Panchgani.

Rather like Great Malvern nestling in the slopes of the Malvern Hills on the opposite side of the world, Panchgani was a town of schools. There were four main ones, two for girls and two for boys and the five boys mentioned earlier were bound for their first term at St. Peter's. Panchgani was a hill station, a place of refuge for those of delicate constitution and sufficient means who wanted to escape the heat of the summer plains below. Ten years after India's partition and independence, there were still a lot of English of Paul Scott's *Staying On* variety in this small town of some three thousand souls, living out their time in the idyllic surroundings of this quiet and peaceful setting from which the view took in the whole panorama of the hill slopes down to the teeming, bustling plain below. The climate was good; it was a paradise in which to live and a wonderful atmosphere in which to grow up as a child in a boarding school.

The five boys met as they left the train at Poona and then took the long, slow bus ride from Poona to their school. Bruce Murray, Farang Irani and Victory Rana were three of the boys. Victory Rana – there's a name! He was a relation of a king and if ever any of us had heard an exotic name before, it couldn't have been half as fanciful as Victory. But as fancy goes, Victory wasn't half the name that another of us was later to adopt. The fourth boy was me, Derrick Branche and the fifth among us had come the longest way to attend school. Faroukh Bulsara had crossed an entire ocean, from Zanzibar, in fact, where he lived with his family. I can't remember whether his sister was also at one of the girls' schools in Panchgani but suffice to say that I remember very well that first time of meeting that fifth member of our company who was later, as you've obviously guessed, to become better known as Freddie Mercury.

DAVID MINNS

I first met Freddie at the beginning of 1975. I think it was March or April although I can't be sure. I had been working for Paul and Linda McCartney for some time, firstly with Vincent Romeo and latterly with Brian Brolly. Paul had just produced an album for his brother, Mike, of *Scaffold* fame, called simply *McGear*, which had been re-leased on Warner Brothers and I was at that time heavily involved with the daily management of Mike's career.

I had also been asked by Chrysalis to manage a singer-song-writer called Eddie Howell and on the night in question, I had taken him to dinner at Fergus Provan's restaurant in the Fulham Road, just next to the cemetery. We came out of the restaurant into the chilly night air. Across the street was another restaurant I was later to get to know very well called September. Coming out of September was Freddie and his old friend Malcolm Grey whom I knew. Freddie's car, driven by Roy Thomas Baker, was parked at the kerb outside Provan's just ahead of the car I was using.

As Freddie and Malcolm crossed the street, there was no mistak-ing the lead singer of *Queen* who after only three albums had made such a name for himself with songs like *Seven Seas of Rye* and *Killer Queen*. Freddie was also making a name for himself in the glam rock stakes and my memory of him that night is indelible. He was wearing the famous fox fur jacket and skintight black satin jeans with white Dr. Scholl clogs. It was the same jacket he wore in the video of *Bohemian Rhapsody*. In fact, the jacket rarely left his back for the first twelve months I knew him. Black-painted finger nails and the Mexican silver snake bangle tastefully accompanied the ensemble and the whole was topped with a haze of carefully teased hair. Freddie was never without his hairbrush which lived in the fox fur jacket. The three of them were inseparable.

This sounds as though I was transfixed by the vision of the approaching rock phenomenon and I suppose I must have been, for I was still on the kerbside as Malcolm introduced us all and we chatted for a few minutes about this that and nothing in particular before Malcolm asked Eddie and I if we wanted to join them at Rod's, a club next to the Furniture Cave past World's End in the Kings Road. Malcolm claused the invitation by saying that Freddie was down in the dumps and needed cheering up. Eddie politely declined and dropped me off at Rod's before going home to an early bed. Roy Thomas Baker also made his way back to the studio. As *Queen*'s producer, his life was virtually lived at the control desk.

For those of you who remember Rod's, Malcolm, Freddie and I sat at the side at a table for four, opposite the long bar and we chatted for what seemed like hours. As it was Freddie who needed cheering up, I felt I ought to let him set the pace of the conversation and indeed he told me mainly about the recordings which were by this time quite

17

well advanced and which by the end of the year would constitute *Queen*'s fourth album, *A Night at the Opera*. I remember him telling me before we said goodbye that night that he often despaired of ever seeing it finished as the recordings had been going on for so long, Brian May having been recently quite ill. It was his confidence that seemed to be dented and this was bringing him down as I found out. I could not help reacting on a personal level to this somewhat battered artiste who had apparently grasped a perfect stranger in order to pour out his woes.

However, professionally, I assured him he really had nothing to worry about, and to not allow private feelings of self-doubt to get in the way of what was obviously going to be a major career.

Though it must seem vast to an outsider, the music business is at its core one of the smallest and closely knit industries that exists under the canopy of entertainment. I was lucky to be working at the very hub of the business in my capacity at McCartney Productions. *The Beatles*, Paul and *Queen* shared EMI as a record label and I had been hearing about the fabulous things predicted for Freddie and *Queen* for some time and so felt as confident as I could that I wasn't bullshitting Freddie as I urged him on encouragingly. At first he seemed to react well to my supportiveness.

However, I was later to discover that he was subject to powerful changes of mood which although were often over as quickly as they came, nonetheless happened regularly. Euphoria could turn to gloom as easily as day turned into night but, strangely, it was in some of his darkest moods that Freddie found his most powerful inspiration both creatively and politically.

For some reason, I had helped dispel the gloom and he put his arm around me and kissed me on the cheek. I was taken aback that someone of Freddie's high profile should behave so affectionately in the middle of the public bar of a crowded club but then I was later to discover that Freddie kissed everyone at the drop of a hairbrush! Remember, it was in the days that men didn't kiss each other too much in public! What was OK for a footballer was definitely not the macho thing for a rock 'n' roll star.

"You look shocked, dear!" Freddie remarked and appeared to be rather pleased with himself for being shocking was one of his favourite pieces of mischief.

We exchanged telephone numbers, his for the time being at Bronze Studios up at the Roundhouse in Chalk Farm and he told me to call him.

It was not until three or four weeks later that I picked up the phone. He was delighted that I'd called.

"Come over tomorrow," he said.

"Great," I said. "Do you mind if I bring Adrienne with me?"

"Adrienne?"

"Posta," I replied. I was seeing a great deal of Adrienne and her then husband Graham Bonnet who was going through a particularly tortuous time of life both personally and professionally and whom I had also been asked to steer.

Adrienne and I arrived at the Bronze Studios. All the members of *Queen* were there. The atmosphere was quite relaxed and they were all very friendly and talkative.

"Now, dear," announces Freddie, "listen to *this* and tell me what you think of my rhapsody! It's not quite finished yet but you'll get the idea."

Roy Thomas Baker's finger hit the play button and what followed was the first time I heard *Bohemian Rhapsody*. When it was over, Freddie was giggling.

"Well?"

"Do you think we can get away with it being so long?" I seem to remember Brian asking.

"It'll either be merely a modest hit or it'll be number one for weeks and weeks," I said. *Queen's* established following was such that I knew chart entry for even as way out a piece as *Bohemian Rhapsody* was pretty certain but I think that everyone that night in that studio knew that it was indeed something rare and special we had just heard.

DAVID EVANS

Freddie came into my life via my flatmate, David Minns. It was early in 1975, which had not started as a particularly memorable year.

I had been working since 1970 for Barry Krost who headed an artists management company in Curzon Street whose major clients were such as Cat Stevens, Colin Blunstone, Peter Finch, Angela Lansbury, Mike Hodges the film director; an excellent list. Barry had moved to Los Angeles permanently in 1974 leaving me to run the London end of what was a pretty significant company, a hybrid in the industry as it straddled so many disciplines; music, acting, directing, writing. It was exciting, glamourous by association and rewarding in an experiential sense. The money, contrary to what could be believed, was lousy.

Thanks to my parents, I had bought a two bedroomed maisonette in Werter Road, off Putney High Street and I shared it, as I had done two previous flats, with David Minns. Though we were never intimate, we were very close friends. We also worked in the same industry, he for the McCartneys. Most of our friends, both performers and people from agency, management, publishing and record companies, came from that world; work and play overlapped. It was a great life for two young men in their twenties, working in the music capital of the world and with that industry's major names. We thought we were without a care.

I was very pleased for David when he first started seeing Freddie on a regular basis. At first, I was only too happy when Freddie started spending more and more time at the flat. That he was mercurial, sorry, has to go without saying but, despite the occasional rages and simmering depressions, he was ninety percent of the time funny, witty, highly intelligent and we shared a love of style, art, movies and show business in general. Also, he didn't have much money in those days either and because we started off as equals in that area, our friendship was never touched by the vast imbalance that was soon to occur when he became so successful. He was ruthlessly self-critical and a meticulous and fastidious perfectionist. He was the sort of man you're thrilled to have as your friend but desperately relieved not to have to wake up next to on a bad morning.

All the stars I've ever had any truck with seem to have that knack of getting you to do things for them and, whether it was a conscious facility or not, Freddie had it in abundance. He also had an unstoppable dynamism about him which made you realise that you should really take care never to get in the way. He wouldn't mow you down on purpose but his juggernaut had already mystically acquired its own momentum.

Bohemian Rhapsody saw Freddie and *Queen* catapulted into the household word kind of celebrity. The 'Queen Mary' Daimler was replaced by a chauffeur driven Silver Shadow Rolls Royce which sat outside the house so often that local children would come knocking on the door for autographs. Endearing the first time, amusing the fifth, bloody infuriating the umpteenth.

The implications of this sea change in all our fortunes were only complicated when I decided to leave Barry Krost's company and set up on my own. I had quite a few clients such as Peter Straker, Brian Protheroe amongst them and Crispin Campbell Lowe was kind enough to sub me with office space. My new found independence was short-lived. John Reid, Elton's manager whom I had known for several years as a friend, had just signed *Queen* for management and, presumably knowing that I knew Freddie, invited me to join his management office. I imagine part of his reason was that I could mop up, should any blood be spilt after the meeting of the two mega-acts, Elton and *Queen*. Presumably, *Queen* or Freddie must have been consulted about my appointment and anyway, I started.

Soon, of course, with *Queen* touring very successfully and *Bohemian Rhapsody* proving such an enormous hit, not only did I have Freddie in the office, I also had him at home. Professionally, Freddie was great. Even after heated meetings in the office when the hackles on the fox would rise and fur would fly, on the way out he would wink at me as if to say: "Didn't mean it personally, dear. See you later."

I knew with a sigh that I was indubitably to see him later and, shame to report, I would groan inwardly, knowing I would have to tread carefully that evening at home as events were rehashed and rearranged. I always found my loyalties badly torn between my employer and his clients.

So, strange to say, I saw Freddie as a kind of threat to the stability of my out-of-office life as I realised that if he and David continued the closeness of their relationship, David would be soon moving out of my flat and I would be left alone. It was a prospect I had not even contemplated. I had merely assumed David and I would get old together and end up in twin bathchairs on the promenade at Eastbourne.

Not unlike a concerned parent, I tackled Freddie late one night in a strange hotel when the band were on the road.

"What," I demanded, "are your intentions? Are you serious about this part of your life? I have to know for it affects me deeply."

Freddie was not only honest, he said he was very serious and events proved him to be, and not only sincere, but declared that he was very concerned for me. He realised what was happening to me for, in an odd way, in order for him to pursue his new-found private life, he had to hurt other people. Personally, I always found him to be never anything less than honest, always sincere and always aware of his responsibilities contingent to his actions. I have to emphasise these qualities because a star's behaviour can sometimes appear, to those who do not understand, whimsical and cruel.

Though I knew I had found a real friend, I was always respectful of Freddie's power. Not the power of his influence nor his wealth but of a certain atavistic, primitive – I hate to use the word but I have to – magical magnetism he exuded which would and did draw people into his vortex. He always knew what *he* was in for when he met new friends but I doubt many of them did.

EDDIE HOWELL

The first time I really remember having any knowledge of Freddie was at Thursday's Club in Kensington which we had booked through the good offices of Moira Bellas. At Warner Brothers Records, I was due to perform the *Eddie Howell Gramophone Record*, my first album for Warners and the band behind me consisted of Robin Lumley on keyboards, Jack Lancaster on sax, Ritchie Dharma on drums, Tony Sadler on guitar and lil ol' me, heading up on accoustic guitar.

Lots of luminaries were due to attend the launch of this album but to my amazement Phil Collins turned up with his congas just before we were due on and joined the band. We played for about twenty minutes, about four tracks of the album when all of a sudden the power blew and the remainder of the hour and a half set seemed in jeopardy. Most of the instruments however still functioned acousti-cally and just when we were going to go on with the set, Derek Taylor, the ex-*Beatles* press officer and then managing director of Warners got up on stage effectively to close the show down. Sud-denly we heard Phil's congas roll to herald what turned out to be a very successful accoustic performance.

I came off stage and the first people I bumped into were David Minns, my manager, and Freddie. Instead of going out to pump the industry flesh as would have been expected of a nascent star on his debut, I was hived off into a corner where Freddie and David were holding court. Over drinks we chattered about what we were going to do after the show and we duly headed off to the White Elephant on the River with Kenny and Lee Everett. We didn't really talk about music much.

"This is Eddie's night," Freddie told everyone and I felt really flattered and made me feel like someone really special, quite content to take very much a backseat after the success of my little show. I later learned that when things had gone awry, Freddie had very much wanted to get up on stage and help out to keep the momentum of the showcase going although he decided not to steal Phil Collins' or my thunder when it was obvious that Phil's help was all that was needed.

PETER STRAKER

It was 1975. David Evans, my then manager, and I were at Provan's restaurant having yet another endless meeting about my ailing career. After having forced David to manage me whilst he was working at Barry Krost's office, he now found himself in yet another quandary for having taken up the complicated yoke of the management of my career, David had just started working for John Reid to help out with the management of really complicated careers.

Coincidentally, Freddie and John Reid were dining at another table in the same restaurant. It was the time when Freddie and John Reid were having a lot of little meetings at the time of *Queen*'s changeover of management from the Sheffield brothers to John. So, that night in Provan's, everyone was having endless little meetings.

David and I were very involved as things were very intense in my career and I hadn't noticed who else was in the restaurant... I'm lying. What I should say is that my vanity prevented me from wearing either spectacles or contact lenses at the time and so there was *no way* I could see who else was in the restaurant. Eventually, John came across to say hello and goodbye as he and Freddie left. John introduced me to Freddie Mercury from *Queen*. The name meant something to me but not a great deal as it had only been *Killer Queen* with which I could identify.

I remember the ratty fur and the black-painted finger nails, the white clogs and the hair. There was also the characteristic hunching of his posture, a slight stoop. However, the real impression with which I was left was his extraordinary shyness. He kept his eyes to the ground, something he always did throughout his life when he was first introduced to strangers. Although I grew to know what the downcast eyes meant, it was that almost painful shyness which I first remember about Freddie.

CAROLINE BOUCHER

It shocks and appals me to confess that I cannot remember meeting Freddie for the first time. I cannot think why he didn't make a huge initial impression on me but he didn't or else I would have remembered. I must have been up to my ears with Elton's work when John Reid announced that I had to pull out all the stops in working for his new signing, *Queen*. I can't have been that pleased at such a huge extra workload.

I must have met Freddie in the context of the band first of all and as a woman, initial eye contact and body language were only with Roger and Brian. Roger related to everyone physically – Brian was large and friendly and, as I recall, only too eager to please. I regret to say that I was repelled, as a woman, by Freddie's appearance. The hair with the split ends, his teeth; his very physical presence was just not one which appealed to me. This had nothing to do with his sexuality as I didn't know it then and got no vibe about it either way and in any case, I worked for Elton who was gay and whom I adored. Of course, as soon as I saw Freddie perform, on stage, he transcended his physical self and metamorphosed, going from chrysalis to butterfly, amazing me that I was watching the same person, showing that you should never judge people by their appearance.

What I do remember about Freddie as soon as I had met him was that he stood very much on ceremony. I got the feeling that he maintained himself at a distance from whoever he was talking to. He was always somewhat elevated from the rank and file of goings on and this was often confusing as he would suddenly, even after laughing and kidding for some time, pull rank and spoil the bonhomie of the   atmosphere which was difficult for all of us as we were ensconced in close proximity promoting *Night at the Opera* around the country in a tour bus. We would all sit around one of the coach's tables and talk for hours and then, pouf! Freddie would be gone. Off, sitting by himself. I remember him travelling then with his own private masseur... poor boy! What a dance Freddie led him although the boy got his own back by telling Freddie the story whilst he pummelled and pushed at the Mercury body that when attending to a famous French film star of the Bardot ilk, he, the masseur, misplaced one of her silicone implants which promptly left her chest to take up residence below her chin! Freddie was terrified for that occasion at least and temporarily relented his torture of the masseur. He was often cat and mouse like that, playing quite cruelly with people he knew couldn't fight back and even those who could.

However, after I left John Reid's to have my first baby, I didn't see Freddie again until a reception a few weeks after my daughter Katie's birth when my husband and I took the little baby in her carrycot to September restaurant in the Fulham Road. We left the baby upstairs in the manager's office whilst we enjoyed a brief respite from nursery fatigues. People were dutiful in enquiring after the baby but basically indifferent. What absolutely amazed me was that the only person who was constantly solicitous, forever going upstairs to check whether Katie was crying or sleeping, was Freddie Mercury.

ANNIE NIGHTINGALE

I was doing a programme called *Sounds of the Seventies* on Wednesday nights with Alan Black. I remember *Queen's* first single, *Seven Seas of Rhye* as it lay on my desk. I can even remember what it looked like. Half red and half beige, from EMI. We'd been listening to new records and that first single made such an impact on me. It was so good, so different. I knew straightaway that they were going to be pretty huge. Like when I played the first *Police* record, I didn't know who they were but I just knew... that kind of thing is very exciting.

You have no idea how much of an effect your own enthusiasm has on a band you are raving about because you have never met them. When you commit to a band and that commitment lasts, as long of course as they keep making good records, all of us really stick with that band. In those days, 'we' also included Bernie Andrews, an amazing stalwart to many a band who owe a great deal to his early support.

I remember reading in *Queen's* biog which accompanied the press kit for the single that they had degrees and that rather impressed me. Though bands are supposed to pay their dues and slog about the country for ages, *Queen* seemed to make it relatively quickly. From the photo that came with the biog, I remember Roger striking me as very pretty. It was Brian and his guitar work who emerged initially as the front runner in the band as far as we in the office were concerned. Freddie wasn't really in there at the beginning. That was before we'd seen them. As soon as we saw them live, we all thought he was wonderfully outrageous although that quality developed slowly. He wasn't all that over the top at the beginning and strangely there wasn't much of a hint that it would be that direction he would follow in his performance style.

By the time *Brighton Rock* came around, I was even more hooked. I am an unashamed Brighton person. I live there and I live there because of Graham Green's *Brighton Rock*. So, as far as I was concerned, anyone who brings out a song called *Brighton Rock* has got my vote.

When it happened, I can't remember but there came a time when Freddie suddenly came out. He jumped out of the band and started to take over. What first to me started as a band, a unit, eventually developed into an entirely different animal by the time *Bohemian Rhapsody* was released. I thought that a very daring move to put out a seven minute single. Its comparable to me to *Boomtown Rats' I Don't Like Mondays*. Both it and *Bo Rhap* could have been a hideous failure. *Queen* seemed to be risking everything, courting professional suicide. Though I've always felt fairly isolated in the taste stakes at the Beeb, I was doing my first Sunday afternoon request show and I played *Bo Rhap* confidently, based on its quality as I try to do with all records. Of course the big breakthrough came with the video for

Bohemian Rhapsody, that incredibly original prismatic effect that Bruce Gowers achieved. It started the whole video revolution. It was a real milestone and a milestone for Freddie for in the video he was singled out visually as the driving force. That said, the band seemed to reach a sort of maturity then. When I go and see a band I always wait to see which member it is who is drawing me, attracting my attention the most. After *Bohemian Rhapsody* that person as far as *Queen* was concerned, was undeniably Freddie.

NINA MYSKOW

I remember being absolutely terrified the first time I met Freddie. It wasn't so much 'met' but merely being in the presence. Upstairs in Mr Chow's restaurant in Knightsbridge after *Queen*'s free gig in Hyde Park in 1977.

I was still living in Scotland, in St Andrews and was editor of *Jackie*, the teenage magazine. I'd been in Edinbugh the night before and John Reid, decreeing that I had to be at the gig the next day, flew me down. John also arranged for me to stay with Sarah Forbes, his then fiancée and I was feeling very swept away with all this particular attention. It seemed like fairy godmother time to me - there was no hint of it being a part of work. I was thrilled, delighted and excited about going to such a special concert under such special circumstances . I did feel then rather out of the way of things, stuck in Scotland.

Kiki Dee was supporting *Queen* and with her we sat in the back of an old van, starting off at Montpellier Square, John Reid's house, to get through the crowds backstage. I remember being overwhelmed as much by the circumstances of the occasion as surprised by how impressed I was by *Queen* as performers, and in particular Freddie.

After the concert, we walked across the park in the dark, John, Sarah and I to Mr Chow's and we all sat round a large circular table upstairs. Mary was there and I can remember Tim Curry was there too. No one bothered to explain to me who Mary was although I obviously knew who Tim was. Freddie joined us later. I remember how disdainfully he looked at me. He gave me 'the look', that visual version of Lady Bracknell's withering 'handbag' and I began to get a bit paranoid. I began to feel that I had no right to be there and self-conscious that I only worked for a naff teenage magazine. He was never properly introduced to me but then I don't suppose he wanted to be. At the end of the evening, John dispatched Sarah and I to her parents' house in Elm Place off Fulham Road. I suppose my first impression of Freddie was of a very daunting star. You couldn't see him any other way than as a star.

MIKE MORAN

April 1986... It was a f...ing hurricane!

He burst into the studio at Abbey Road where I was working on the *Time* album. Dave Clark, *Time's* producer, had told me that Freddie had agreed to sing a couple of tracks on the album and thought he and I would get on very well together.

Freddie had been spending a lot of time in Germany, but he was on the point of leaving Munich for good and returning to England. The day before our first scheduled session, I was driving back home and had a head-on collision with a lorry. The car was a write off and I broke four ribs and hurt both wrists! I couldn't have been in worse shape. I let Dave know I'd had a 'slight' car accident but that I was okay. I dosed myself up with a few painkillers but turned up at Abbey Road feeling and looking like death. I begged Dave not to tell Freddie...

In he came, along with the retinue – Straker, etc... Looking very macho with T-shirt and calling for refreshments he strode up to me and said:

"What's the matter with you? The girl looks positively peaky!"

He forced me to have a drink of Stolichnaya and somehow we produced a backing track. He really worked me to the bone that day yet he worked hard and constructively. He was in the studio to work and that's what he did. He never goofed off, he took it absolutely seriously and worked from the minute he walked in to the minute he left.

At about two o'clock the following morning, I was fiddling about with a fancy little piece of piano technique, something which Fred always seized on. Fred suddenly said:

"I like that. Do it again!"

At this point in the session I was in a lot of pain and I was exhausted. Dave tried to come to my rescue and explained to Freddie that I was in some pain because I'd been in a car crash the previous day.

"She'll be alright, dear," Freddie replied, brushing aside my condition. "Let's just get on with it. Give her something, give her anything. Just keep her going!"

And on he went, taking things always at his own pace, never anyone else's. He was constantly improving things, always trying to better something which, often, to others' ears could not be bettered. His creative ability was quite shattering. Based on the foundation of trust he appeared to have in my trained background, he worked furiously.

"Write it down for me ... just as I like it."

I would write it down in that peculiar notation he liked. We found out we had a really good way of working. He loved trying everything, even the impossible, battering performances out of anyone he could bully into doing things better and better and better. Again and again and again. His wilder ideas would all have to be tried, as often they would work and would make the difference between something that was passable and something that was unsurpassable.

His two tracks on the *Time* album are truly Freddie renditions. Cliff was quite taken aback when he heard them. His reaction was that his, the Cliff version would be rather different.

Freddie and I were in the Abbey Road studios for perhaps three or four weeks and got on like a house on fire. There was an element of party time to working then but the professionalism was always underlying everything. We became, almost, instant friends. I loved being with him. That lovely house at Logan Place... always lovely.

The video for *Time* was done on the stage at The Dominion Theatre. The shoot was from very early morning and had to be done during the day as the show had to go on in the evening and I was MD'ing it. Freddie, in the evening, instead of going home, decided to become an usherette and started to take round ice creams, shocking the amazed audience. He cared not a jot at being recognised and dealt with customer complaints in a typically blunt way. One outraged woman complained that she hadn't ordered a cornet...

"Stick it..." was the unprintable reply!

Freddie was a Cliff fan. He was very respectful of Cliff's position and especially his starring role in the show and never tried to compete. I know he loved being a part of the project.

JACKY GUNN

Let me think. It was July 1982 at the *Queen* office. Fiona was the girl who I was working with and we were both very new. We were excited. Vicky, our predecessor, led me to believe that Freddie never wanted to meet the new staff and told me so rather dismissively. I rather thought he might be an ogre. But anyway, I still primped myself a bit in anticipation.

Much to Vicky's annoyance, Freddie rang down and wanted to meet us. Up the stairs we went. Fiona was a giantess and when he shook hands with us and welcomed us to the team, he realised he was standing on a lower step to her. He quickly corrected this so that she was properly in his perspective. He was really sweet and told us if we had any problems to come to him! The build-up to meeting him was huge. It was conveyed to us that he was terrifying. My first impression was how quiet he was and how well-spoken. He seemed very shy. I got to know that this shyness, this almost aloof politeness, was something that others interpreted as snobbish but it was never ever a feeling I had from him. He was entirely different from the others in the band who were much more social. Freddie was never one for a pint in the Sun in Splendour, our pub across the road. I once mentioned it and he looked at me as though I was insane.

There was a lot of touring after that. The band were all over the world. We even got a postcard from Japan.

"Hello, dears. Here we are!"

JIM JENKINS

First impression was seeing him on *The Old Grey Whistle Test*. I thought he was really weird – the long hair and the black nails. A short time later I went to see the band who were supporting *Mott the Hoople* and I was fascinated. Obviously, the focal point of a band is the lead singer and so I suppose I was picking up on Freddie more than any of the others. Gone were the T-shirts I'd seen them in on the telly and in were the black and white costumes. There was a lot of contradiction about him. *Liar* was so vicious and so hard and yet when he spoke after the song, in between the songs, he was entirely different, so quiet.

I didn't see *Queen* again for ages but when they came back to Liverpool, I plucked up courage and found out where they were staying. I went down the hotel corridor and knocked on the door of his room. Mary answered and asked what I wanted. I asked to see Freddie and before she could say anything, there was a booming voice from inside the room:

"What do you want?"

I explained, that I just wanted to meet him. Out he came and he was really nice. I had a huge pile of things to sign.

"You want me to sign all *these*!" He only sounded outraged and he signed every single one.

I later became a real fan, joined the club. When Theresa joined the fan club organisation, they contacted me as I had lots of information on the history of *Queen*. Concerts, telly appearances, that sort of stuff. I kept everything and I've got a really good memory for dates and things.

At Alexandra Palace, I approached him to ask for an autograph thinking truly he'd forgotten who I was.

"Is it for you?" he asked. I nodded. He signed: "To Jim," without asking what my name was. I was really chuffed. I grabbed my friend Dave Walmsley's arm. Dave took lots of *Queen* photos.

"He remembered me," I said. "He remembered who I was."

PAUL GAMBACCINI

It was in Boston, Massachussets. In my brief stint as executive producer of WBZ in Boston, the largest radio station in New England and the only radio station in America with three letters in its signature. *Queen* were in town to launch the *Sheer Heart Attack* album. The launch was held in the bar which is now the *Cheers* bar of TV fame. I was with my assistant Beverly Mire. Freddie was totally chatty and open. Although clearly a star in his demeanour, he was utterly personal. That was always the paradox of Freddie.

GORDON ATKINSON

January 19th 1976. Can't remember what day of the week that was though. I remember this very slinky guy dressed in black leather with long hair and a serpent bracelet being shown into my surgery. He hardly looked at me. He looked at the prints around the walls of the surgery. He knew some of the artists. At first he behaved as though he was in an art gallery, positioning himself in front of each picture and appreciating it before moving on to the next. His voice was quite extraordinary. Very clear speaking voice, very musical. Lovely pronunciation. With a slight lisp. He was extremely shy. But there was a nice reaction between us. I felt as shy as he was.

The next time I saw him socially wasn't for a couple of years when I went to his thirtieth birthday party at Country Cousin which was a magnificent affair. It included a dancer who incorporated some snakes into her somewhat risqué act which was performed on top of one of the tables.

I have to be honest that I didn't understand who he was or what he was about when I first met him and indeed his professional life was never anything to do with our friendship. At the beginning, I thought he was very Biba-ish, very Carnaby Street. His hands were forever flickering and waving as he emphasised whatever it was he was saying.

You always got that feeling that he was manipulating you, producing the effect he wanted. In the nicest possible way, you knew you would never have to think of anything for the rest of the time you were due to be with him. He thought everything through for you, putting you at the centre of whatever production it was he was involved in whether it be a dinner or a party, an outing to the opera or the ballet.

However, he made his mind up about you very quickly. He looked and decided within seconds whether he wanted to even speak another word to you. Very intelligent person, quietly studying and assimilating everything around him.

DAVID MUNNS

Queen used to hang around the office a lot at Manchester Square. Joop Visser signed the band. He was the head of A & R. The band were brought in during the Gerry Oord era. Freddie came in quite a few times to see Gerry and Joop. That's where I first met him.

Very few people liked *Bohemian Rhapsody* at EMI. They thought *Queen* had gone mad. But the secretaries liked it. All the girls liked it. After a bit of discussion about "how can you do an edit?" – yes, they actually talked about it – EMI put it out as it was.

I was very young at the time, only about 24 and all I know is that *Bo Rhap* sounded alright to me. It was one of those records in life which made a difference to the whole record business. There've only been two or three in my whole life. That, and *Anarchy in the U.K.* from *the Sex Pistols*. Those records made people change their attitude to the whole business. Then the video. It was less than ten grand but more than our whole annual budget for videos in those days. We had a heart attack when we saw the cost. On paper, the record should never have been a hit. Too long, too camp... Then *Top of the Pops* played it uncut and it was out there – a hit. It did me a lot of good, I know that.

Freddie occasionally called up Bob Mercer and asked us down to the studio. He let us in on the work he was doing and played us what he thought were the hits. If we didn't like something, he'd be fine about us saying that. He used to get very impatient with people if you were just saying what you thought he wanted to hear. I just used to say what I thought, not what I thought he wanted to hear.

We really did roll the boat out for *Bo Rhap* though. It was the record of the year and by the time *Night at the Opera* came out in January 1976, it was huge. I'd come across *Queen* before when I was at EMI International but hadn't had a lot to do with them. Bob Mercer was the other man who had a lot to do with *Queen*. I had worked on *Sheer Heart Attack* before as I was trying to liase with the American company, Capitol Records, about the British catalogue, trying to get them to take as much as I could get them to.

At the Hyde Park gig in September 1976, it was all a bit crazy. Butterflies flew out of fridges. Stuff like that. By that time, the band were on a roll and in a way no one at EMI really knew what to do with them. Freddie at this point realised that all the doors had unlocked, all the lights had come on and he'd got the angle. All the bugs had been ironed out and he was just going to go with it. He'd established all the elements of the rock side of the band and he was sorting out the theatricals. The puzzle had turned into a real picture for him. He knew he was the captain of the ship now.

PETER HINCE

I should mention that when I first started working for *Queen* I acquired the nickname 'Ratty'. I had been called The Rat and it was later commuted to Ratty. When I started in the business, I was only about seventeen and they made me crawl in the smallest spaces between the stacked equipment and the roof of the trucks. Hence, The Rat. Also, I had extremely long greasy hair and was covered in dirt from all that crawling around. When told that a new roadie had been acquired for him, Freddie asked who it was:

"Ratty" they said.

"I shall call him Peter," Freddie announced grandly but it didn't last long.

The first time I met him was at rehearsals for the *Mott the Hoople* U.K. tour which was *Queen*'s first big English tour. They were supporting. It was November 1973. They were promoting *Queen 1.* The rehearsals were at Manticore which was *Emerson Lake and Palmer*'s premises at the old cinema on Fulham Broadway and Northend Road. *Queen* came in halfway through to do their bit and that was when I was first aware of Freddie and the band. *Mott* was a rock'n'roll band and very much jeans and T-shirts for rehearsals. *Queen* came in and they were all dressed up in costume. It was still the glam rock thing and their appearance caused a few remarks like,

"Who *are* these guys?"

From day one they were very demanding. They had to have a drum riser when no other support act would have been granted one. Lots of other things. They seemed to arrive out of nowhere. They hadn't paid their dues as I would call it, hadn't trucked up and down the motorway for example. It all seemed very calculated. Someone had put their money where their mouth was. *Queen* were definitely being pushed. They were difficult, though, seeing that they were only a support band to *Mott* who were pretty big then. *Mott* and *Queen* got on very well though, appreciating each other as musicians and performers. *Queen* learned a lot from *Mott* in the way of profession-alism and stuff like that.

The very first gig of that tour was at Leeds City Hall. I remember the end of the tour too at Hammersmith Odeon. There were two shows and it was a big showpiece for *Queen*. The band wasn't good and seemed to blow it, blew all the good work they'd been doing on the tour.

To be honest, everyone thought that Freddie was a bit of a wally. Even though it was glam, Freddie was over the top even for that. All that flowing costume stuff. I didn't think he was particularly the strongest then. They were all very much a unit.

FIRST IMPRESSIONS

GARY LANGAN

This person in black satin trousers with the top button undone – always that top button undone, with the finger nails on his left hand painted black, always immaculately applied – walked in. He had long black hair then. He was the first person I'd ever seen wearing make-up during the day. I thought that was truly outrageous. I was only seventeen and a half then, from Wimbledon. He'd come in to the studio at Sarm East in the morning and sit down and stay in that same chair all day long. He'd just stay there. We'd start work about twelve o'clock and he wouldn't move. There they were Rag, Tag and Bobtail – Roy Thomas Baker, Freddie and Mike Stone.

There was something commanding there, something about being in command. You looked at this man and sort of knew that he and *Queen* were going to be something huge. We mixed *Keep Yourself Alive* and *Now I'm Here*. It was the first real rock album I'd worked on.

Freddie had powerful moods. He went from quiet and saying nothing to great vocal extravaganzas in the studio, saying what should be done. The other band members were always around of course, in the studio but Freddie was always there at the desk. I thought he was quite frightening as a person, quite awesome. Even then his charisma was larger than life. He wasn't very approachable. If you were going to be his friend, you knew it was going to be something you had to work on. A friendship with Freddie was not something that he was going to accept after a glance.

CHRIS TAYLOR

Like Ratty, I have a nickname. It's Crystal. Short for Chris Taylor. I got it when I was working for *Merlin* and it stuck. I met Ratty whilst we were both working for David Essex. So, I'm Crystal.

I first met *Queen* at John Reid's office in South Audley Street at *Bo Rhap* time. I'd had a call from Ritchie, the guitar roadie, asking if I'd like to go to Japan, Australia and America with *Queen* for three months. I'd agreed immediately.

Brian was the first to walk in. Looked like a praying mantis. Clogs and stuff and stood on my foot and spent the next fifteen minutes apologising. Freddie then walked in and said:

"Very pleased to meet you, dear."

Not the butchest bloke in the world I thought. Still, I was then taken off to Roger's bedsit in Barnes. As I was supposed to be going to be his roadie, Ritchie thought it was obviously an idea for me to meet him. There he was with his shoulder length bleached blonde hair looking like Debbie Harry. He said 'Hello' in a very high pitched voice and I thought, 'Hello, they're *all* fags!"

We didn't mix on that first tour. We were us and they were them. The band turned up for sound checks wearing the full thing, like they were going to do the show then and there. It was very much them and us.

BILLY SQUIER

I first met Freddie in Boston in, probably, 1974. It was around the time of the launch of *Queen II*. Anyway, it was the first time the band had come to America.

I was involved with a formidable Boston DJ at the time; she was a real champion of the music scene, always promoting awareness of new bands so naturally she always got the latest releases from the record companies. *Queen I* came through her mailbox and that's how I was introduced to *Queen*.

The name, I thought, was quite bizarre for a 'rock band', evoking some obvious gay associations. The reference to royalty was somewhat lost as in America we have no queen. The photos on the sleeve too I thought pretty provocative; those shots of Freddie with his painted nails and his pussy cats. Though I personally wasn't put off, I can acknowledge that in those days of the early seventies, a guy with painted finger nails, and black painted nails at that, was pretty unusual. Anyway, being a musician and aspiring rock star myself, I was naturally curious about something so dramatically different than what was then perceived as the 'norm', and so put on the record... and what a difference it was! In many ways, the music seemed contrary to the initial impression created by the cover, though in retrospect the aural drama of the disc was very well matched to the visual pyrotechnics.

We were invited to the album launch and afterwards, my girl-friend and I were invited out to dinner; it was just us, the guys from *Queen* and a couple of people from the record company.

We went to this restaurant, and the way the seating worked out, I wound up next to Freddie. I remember it perfectly: Freddie was wearing white satin pants, very, very tight fitting, along with some sort of brocade jacket. He looked very rakish. As we went to sit down, I can still picture him looking round rather furtively, as if to make sure no one was watching and then he quietly undid his trousers and quickly took his seat. I immediately realized that his 'costume' prevented him from sitting comfortably. It was very unexpected and I thought quite humorous to see Mr. Mercury exposed (not literally) in this way. I don't know if he realized at the time, but I kept his secret (at least for the moment).

I can't even remember them drinking at all in those days. They were really quiet and low-key, not at all how their music might have led me to perceive them. Freddie struck me as being very composed and rather an enigmatic sort of presence. I found it hard to believe that the music I'd just listened to had emanated from the same band I was having dinner with. Their demeanour, especially Freddie's, was so totally different to how they performed on stage.

TONY HADLEY

First time I ever met Freddie and the rest of the guys was during the *Works* tour at Birmingham NEC. I got my office to ring for tickets for my wife and myself. We got backstage passes too. I'd grown up with *Queen* and to eventually get to meet the band and Freddie was great. I met the guys generally just backstage. With Freddie, I don't know, you were sort of summoned... He kind of held court. He was there in his dressing room. He was really, really polite. He was pacing up and down, quite nervous. Very precise and very controlled because he was just about to go onstage. I was overawed. Without a doubt, when you met him you knew you were meeting a star. Freddie knew that too... He knew he was in control.

After the show there was a party. With *Queen* there was always a party. Freddie was there smoking like a trooper. I walked in. He patted the seat next to him and said, ignoring my wife:

"Come and sit next to Freddie, dear. We're going to have some fun tonight, darling!"

Meeting someone who was an idol, someone whom I'd always respected as a musician and a singer was great. Being a singer too, it was a great thrill for me. The great thing about this business is that there are special high points. Freddie, Bowie, Elton, Eric Clapton; people whom you've grown up with and have been a great influence on your life, to meet them, it really is a high point. Freddie was one of the biggest stars. He loved being a star and playing the star. I've learned from that. He's given me advice about it and it's been good advice.

TIM RICE

I didn't get to meet Freddie until he was a big star. I was definitely musically impressed fairly early on. *Seven Seas of Rhye* I thought was OK but *Killer Queen* I really thought superb. In the early days of *Queen* I was working at Capital Radio and I must say that *Bo Rhap* was one of those records you get about ten a decade of. I remember I was driving to my sister-in-law's and this record came on, this six and a half minute song. I was only three minutes away from her gate and I had to turn round and retrace my wheels in order to be able to hear it complete! The video was superb too. From then on, I knew that *Queen* was a band to watch.

One of the great things about Freddie was that he was very much a part of a band. He was quite happy to work like that with three guys who were equally talented. Often you find that the front man walks away after a while. But he was there with the others who were also writers and performers which is often forgotten. They all did their solo projects but I feel that his contribution was just as much as a team player as being an individual.

As time wore on and he and the other boys became part of the rock establishment, I wanted to meet them. Slowly but surely I saw them at the occasional function. About 86/87, it came about that as one realised what a superb catalogue they had, that I had an idea with Elaine Paige for her to do an album of their songs and through that we got to meet up, other than passing each other at parties.

Through that I got the chance to write some lyrics for the *Barcelona* album. Elaine and I got to know him very well at that stage. We met at his house a lot and got to know him much more than as a rock performer. He went so much deeper.

The Caballé album was fascinating with that wonderful hit *Barcelona* on it. He proved that you could still go over the top and mean it. In that one album, above all others, he combined sincerity and total extravagance.

There were so many *Queen* songs which said a lot of heavy things and sometimes the seriousness of the songs could be hidden by the extravagant presentations. I realised this when working with Elaine, finding out all the various ways these songs could be sung, songs like *Who Wants to Live for Ever, Love of My Life*. She also did a wonderful version of *Bohemian Rhapsody*. All those songs with, especially at the end, that double meaning if you knew of Freddie's condition.

I've spent a lot of time in the States in the last six months and it's a little sad that although people recognise how great he was, there was a time when America didn't accept him or *Queen*, almost as though he was too theatrical, too English in a way.

Working with him, I found that he was so quiet, in the studio or at home, so softly and quietly spoken. Such a contradiction to the man who took over on stage. He was a very learned and intelligent man, very well-read. He knew a lot about art and travel. He was modest too, he never seemed to want to go out of the way to show off the intellectual side of his character. I was very surprised by the many sides to him, the way he was able to keep his life very personal whereas the flamboyance of his stage presentation was such the opposite.

On the way back from L.A. last week, I chose *Queen Flicks II* as my video choice. Songs that hadn't necessarily come across that well for me on radio, when seen as video or filmic creations are superb.

DIANA MOSELEY

I'd just begun my career and videos in the early 80's were fantastic. Masses of room to experiment. I'd done several videos, the latest three with Boy George, Paul Young and David Bowie. My connection was with David Mallett and Jackie Byford of the MGM production company who worked a lot with *Queen*, notably *Radio Gaga*. The call came for me to work on *Born to Love You*, a Freddie video as opposed to a *Queen* production. My background was with actors; I had a degree in theatre design at Wimbledon School of Art. I was slightly apprehensive that he was considered difficult and it had even been suggested that my path might not be as easy because I was a woman. How wrong that piece of information turned out to be!

I was very worried when I heard that there were going to be about a thousand extras; all girls... I sat in on the initial production meeting. Freddie, the Director, etc... My fears were shortlived as the meeting was very relaxed, feet up, coffees coming and going. Freddie was as excited as I was. Even though he'd been doing it for years, he was thrilled by the grand design and concept of it, a *thousand* girls!

The concept was almost instantly reduced to five hundred... top whack! My sketch pad was soon on my lap and Freddie, I noticed was really interested, peeking at what I was doing at every available moment, fingers and hands twitching, aching to hold a pencil.

I was gleaning this amazing sense of theatre which Freddie was exuding. There was a huge sense of drama coming through. Ideas started spinning and spontaneously I thought of warriors! Etruscan women! Breastplates...

"Yes! Yes!" Freddie exclaimed and instantly fell to his knees and grabbed a pencil from me and we started designing breastplates and helmets and stuff. Freddie and I were having a wonderful time and the poor producers were busy adding up figures, number crunching as the warriors of love, the amazons of love à la Alan Jones took shape with their red, almost heart-shaped breastplates which were beginning to march off my sketchpad. We worked out his costume; a white affair, a little battered because of all the love going around.

"Don't forget my legs are a bit thin, Diana!" Freddie instructed as he was a little nervous that the effect we wanted might not be achieved because of his skinny legs. I explained that I could turn him into a muscle-man if he wanted. The thigh of the costume did end up a little padded, just to outline the muscle contour. His carriage and posture was excellent, almost balletic.

In the end, the costume was wonderful. The vacuum-formed breastplates arrived and Willie Burt the costume cutter for the RSC and the Opera House came in to do Freddie's costume. They hit it off immediately too, thank goodness. Freddie was such a perfectionist. He always wanted something which needed to be made. He never wanted anything which could be bought off the peg as it were.

I remember the first fitting with that particular costume. We were doing a three day shoot, videos being done in a great hurry. It was made up with lycra, more readily fittable. He saw the costume only at the end of the first day which gave me very little time to change anything. The atmosphere was really exciting. Freddie was almost directing the shoot, getting in behind the camera at every opportunity. There was almost a court around Freddie in the dressing room, tons of people but everyone joining in. Eventually he asked to try on the jacket. He leapt out of the make-up chair and almost screamed with excitement.

"I love it, I love it. I want another in leather!"

However when he put on the lower half of the costume, I noticed that there was a slight sag in the crotch area. The bum fit was fabulous but something had to be done about the saggy crotch. I had no male dresser at my disposal and so I had to get out the pins and do the business myself. It was the moment when I got to know Freddie once and for all. My assistants were all peering out wondering what would happen. I unpicked the offending area and then inserted another piece of fabric. Re-fitting them, I just stared him in the eye and ordered him:

"Spread your legs!"

He was so surprised, but before he knew what had hit him, I dived between his legs and grabbed the material and hey presto... everything turned out fine.

In the end we only had three hundred girls. Arlene Phillips choreographed and it was a wonderful shoot and a fabulous production. That was my baptism into the business of working with Freddie.

At the end of the shoot, two French passion dancers – slap your face, violent tango, kiss-and-make-up dancing – had been booked to appear in the last shots. Being thrown about the set, the poor woman who was the female partner ended up being slammed against the side of the set where she lay unconscious, the bump on her head growing by the second. Everyone was thrown into horrified consternation, almost paralysed, not knowing what to do. Immediately, Freddie took charge, the total gallant, and ordered an ambulance, ordered her taken to his dressing room and when the ambulance arrived, off went Freddie in full costume as the white knight of love with her to the hospital.

In the East End, Limehouse way, hospital service was not the quickest, it took a time and while he was waiting for the dancer to be treated, he'd apparently been around the hospital ward, signing autographs, cheering on the troops and cheering everyone up enormously.

After that, at three in the morning, he returned with the previously knocked out passion dancer to finish the sequence. The director called a wrap at five in the morning!

ANN ORTMAN

The very first impression I have of meeting Freddie was going through that little door in Logan Place and walking into that beautiful garden surrounding that equally lovely house. It was such a surprise to find that set-up, in London, although I didn't really know what I had been expecting.

Then I remember Freddie meeting us at the door. He was much smaller than I had previously thought of him from seeing him on television screens and concert stages. He struck me as extremely shy but on the other hand he was very considerate and a very, very good host. I'd been asked to go to have lunch with him because he'd seen a couple of paintings I'd done of a friend's cats and, having then five of his own, he wanted immediately for his darlings to be similarly immortalised. It was Sunday lunch that had eventually been decided on for our meeting and the lunch was traditional – lamb, roast potatoes and all the trimmings. I remember the dining room was painted an extraordinarily intense yellow; not a usual, decorator's yellow. The colour made the room light up. As well as myself at lunch, there was David Evans, Peter Straker, Mary Austin as well as Jim Hutton and Peter and Joe, the guys who lived at the house. I think there was another guest that day, a musician but my memory of him is a bit hazy.

I remember that day Freddie had been both picking flowers from his garden and also choosing from a load of delivered blooms, making selections of shapes and colours and sizes and trying them out in the huge range of his collection of porcelain and glass. He was taking enormous trouble over each arrangement, studying each one for ages, asking people what they thought before being satisfied sufficiently to put the arrangement out on display.

I thought he had the most wonderful skin. I remember it as being peach-like, pinky-brown. What I would call perfect skin.

Of course, cats were all around and I was, after all, there to work with them rather than their owner. The only way I can work with cats is from photographs and so I spent a couple of hours taking photos of them in all sorts of different situations and attitudes. Inevitably though, their anxious owner, almost like a proud parent, crept into the pictures and I'm pleased to say that I have some wonderful photographs of that day to remind me of Freddie, especially ones of him sitting with his cats on his lap.

Every surface in that drawing room including the grand piano seemed to be covered with silver photograph frames, most of them containing pictures of his cats.

I came away at the end of that day, after tea, thinking how much I'd enjoyed it and how much I would like to get to know Freddie more. He was the kind of person you can't forget... I can't describe it, really.

I think I told him I needed a month at least to work my drawings to a point where he could come and see what he thought. Instead of doing only one drawing per cat, I did two and in two cases three so there were twelve half-finished paintings laid out all over the floor of my house in Islington when he came over to see them. The street must have been twittering aloud as that big Mercedes limo pulled up outside. I thought he'd take just five of them but instead he ended up by taking all but one of them and I've kept that one.

When the paintings were finished, I took them over to Logan Place although this was only a short visit. He arranged for them to be framed and when they came back, they hung, so I believe, in his bedroom for a couple of years before he re-arranged things. One of the paintings, a portrait of Oscar, his big ginger tom, was auctioned at a *Queen* fan club convention and sold for upwards of eight hundred pounds! I was delighted. Not only because of the cat herself, but I will always love the song Freddie wrote about Delilah, his tortoiseshell.

TREVOR CLARKE

I first met Freddie in 1975 at Maunkberry's, the famous club in London's Jermyn Street which I managed. Peter Straker, an old friend and regular patron of the club, came in with someone whom I'd never seen before. I react well to people whom I think have something to offer and when I was introduced to Freddie Mercury, my first reaction was:

"And who the hell is Freddie Mercury!"

I shook hands, rather I touched extended fingers, with this person whom I remember as being very little and utterly forgettable. Freddie was not at all what I considered a star in those days, but he was learning, paying great attention to people who did have names and reputations...

As I was later to discover, Freddie and I shared the trait of being somewhat dismissive at times and I hate to admit this but at first, I completely dismissed a person with whom I was later to share so much and whose kindness and friendship were to play a great part in my life. I didn't listen to pop music much and what was played by the DJ at the club was only remarkable if it kept people dancing. In fact, John Reid brought in *Queen*'s next album, *A Day at the Races*. When I enquired whether it was any good, he said:

"Play it!"

I instructed the DJ to play it and the music cleared the dance floor; that spelled instant disaster in a nightclub! No wonder I never really got to meet Freddie until 1978 when I first saw him perform at Earls Court... That huge crown began to emerge from the stage and the band scampered off it... It was marvellous. I was a convert.

I went to Freddie's flat in Stafford Terrace several times before getting anywhere near Freddie. Our friendship was very gradual and never had anything to do with music. Freddie never came at you... You had to go to him but eventually we got to know each other better, then well and finally we became very good friends. Close friends. For a long time, Straker, Freddie and I were inseparable. He paid me an enormous compliment once:

"You know that walk I do, onstage? It's yours, dear!"

Next time I watched him in concert, there was my walk! He told me he used to watch me at work amongst the tables in Maunkberry's and had picked it up from there. He was a great one for looking and learning and turning it into something he made his own.

SARAH STANDING

I don't remember the very first time I met Freddie but I think it was probably when I was seventeen and first started working for John Reid Enterprises, my first ever job. I was completely unqualified as assistant to Caroline Boucher, the press officer. My only qualification was that I knew John Reid and that I was a fan.

I went up to Edinburgh to work on John's Festival of Popular Music at The Playhouse and stayed in a little house John had rented in St Ann's Terrace. I started to see a lot of Freddie as *Queen* had just been signed by John for management.

Freddie was very unflashy but highly intelligent with a very ascerbic wit. He was very unecessarily, as I thought, nice to me as I was completely green and completely overwhelmed not only by my job but also by the fact that I was headily in love with my employer; it was amazing I even noticed anyone else, so consumed and possessed by love was I in the way only a seventeen year old could be.

I thought that Freddie's performance on stage was mind-blowingly wonderful and different and theatrical. I suppose I had a very unrealistic view of the pop world for both he and Elton John, John's other major client, were not the stereotypical rock 'n' roll stars. They merged into the establishment in a very easy way and they were accessible. In retrospect that period was probably pre the drug phase which the industry seemed to sink into and which dragged so many people down with it.

I remember I made my father fly up from Newcastle where he was filming a party political shoot to see *Queen* who were booked into the Festival of Popular Music at the Playhouse. I wanted my father to share my enthusiasm for the performance which, of course he did. I felt proud and vindicated as my father came to see his daughter at work.

I remember going later that summer to the free gig which *Queen* played in Hyde Park. I realised that that concert would be one which would go down in history. It was a beautiful day in September and I remember going afterwards to Mr Chow's in Knightsbridge for dinner. I remember Freddie being incredibly sweet to Mary. He never gave out any specific sexual vibe although his stage act was very sexual in it's almost balletic execution; he exuded almost a pure and non-exclusive form of sexuality, which sort of transcended sex itself but which was appealing to both sexes, straight or gay.

Later on, in 1978, I unwittingly, through being at the right place at the wrong time, found myself party to the break-up of Freddie's relationship with David Minns. Because of the delicate nature of the parting, Freddie was forced in a way to take me into his confidence. I know he was very grateful for what I was able to do for David. I was nothing to Freddie, merely the about-to-be-ex-girlfriend of his soon-to-be-ex-manager but I felt that there was a switch in our

FIRST IMPRESSIONS

relationship after that incident. As he had had no alternative but to trust my integrity, he did just that; he trusted me and I felt we stepped onto a better footing.

He was never flaky to me. Rather rock solid. He was one of the few people who seemed to be genuinely happy when John Reid and I announced our engagement. He had that very necessary 'c'est la vie' and 'whatever-gets-you-through-the-night' approach to relationships. He didn't categorise anybody or pigeonhole them and force them in a box.

SARAH HARRISON

I first met Freddie when I was working for Cat Stevens as his personal assistant.

Having known both David Minns and David Evans since the late sixties when I first worked for Barry Krost, my life has been inextricably tied with theirs, both professionally and as friends from that time until now. I was therefore fortunate to meet Freddie within that relaxed and trusted environment which enabled Freddie to be totally himself.

Being part of a particularly close-knit group of friends, all of us working with stars from the musical and theatrical world, I suppose that the advent of someone as volatile and charismatic as Freddie was registered and then assimilated without too much trauma, although you could be sure that with Freddie there was always a drama round the corner!

The things I remember most about that time was that it was such fun; we were very fortunate to be at the hub of what was happening then and London was fun. As happens with every decade, there are always the 'in' spots and in London in the seventies, the 'in' spot was definitely a place called Rod's, situated in what is now the Furniture Cave at World's End on King's Road Chelsea. Rod's was the first discotheque in London to emulate those of Los Angeles and New York and therefore a magnet for the fun-seeking international set who in turn attracted their own fun friends. Rod's then metamorphosed into Country Cousin, the first proper cabaret and supper club in London, attracting an incredibly wide spectrum of international acts from Holly Woodlawn to Peter Allen, Charles Pierce to Gotham.

It was in this environment that I remember my friendship with Freddie being forged, alongside the people with whom he felt comfortable; it was an environment which created an atmosphere which allowed Freddie free rein to be his natural, wild, funny, outrageous, generous self.

NIGEL QUINEY

A great friend of mine had known Freddie almost from the beginning and so I had some knowledge of him in a way that perhaps I wouldn't have had otherwise. I was not particularly into 'pop' but I had been very impressed with *Bohemian Rhapsody* which had absolutely stood out amongst the other musical offerings at the time.

I was therefore delighted and intrigued when an invitation arrived to attend Peter Straker's birthday party in a Soho restaurant which Freddie was hosting.

I'd never met a pop star before and had no idea what to expect. I suppose I was slightly disappointed that the restaurant was so small and ordinary, having had visions of Freddie taking over vast penthouse nightclubs. However, upon entering a room fairly crammed full of people, kind of noisy and swaying, there was Freddie.

Before I met him, I suppose I was surprised that he was so big, tall. It always had seemed to me that pop and movie stars turned out to be very much smaller in real life than when surveyed on the screen. He also had a tremendous presence which added to his stature. I was introduced and although I don't remember what we talked about, the conversation seemed quite ordinary.

Suddenly, with a flourish of what I now know to be his famous hand movements, he called for a cigarette:

"Ciggy," he commanded.

In moments, cigarette packs appeared for him to take his pick. Wow, I thought... That's stardom and as I smoked myself at the time and as I watched the cigarette being lit for him, how vividly I was reminded of the magical, glamorous allure of the cigarette in the hands of a star. I thought of Bette Davis and her power to manipulate the smoke and the cigarette itself to such great effect for that was exactly what Freddie was doing. I never saw him on stage except on television. He was extraordinary in the way he created and projected the power at his disposal.

A few minutes later, another command was issued:

"Pee pee!"

The same people as bore the cigarettes hustled him away. I turned to my friend and inquired:

"Could pee pee mean lavatory?"

And then I realised that of course it could and did because stars like Freddie have to be protected in public, even, if not especially, in the lavatory. It set my mind racing.

CHERRY BROWN

It was in the first and then the heyday of Country Cousin where I found myself acting as restaurant manager, personnel officer, greeter, bar person... and it was also where I got to meet Freddie.

You have to remember that in those days he was still living with Mary and I suppose that the time had come when he could no longer suppress that part of him which told him and us that he was and wanted to be gay. Freddie had nowhere of his own in those days where he could explore and test that side of himself and so a lot of it had to take place almost in public.

Freddie's first serious attempt at a gay relationship lived in public was therefore played out bathed in the discreet glow of the Country Cousin footlights. People in clubs are great whisperers; gossip is always rife and I had heard for sometime that a close friend was 'going out' with this 'terribly important pop star'.

Club proprietors are as often ignorant of the current tides which are washing this one and that one to their doors and I and Christopher Hunter were no exception. I'd never even *heard* of Freddie Mercury.

However, I can remember two or three days later seeing the *Bohemian Rhapsody* video on television and realising the singer of *Queen* was this same 'terribly important pop star'. I also realised that my friend had become involved with someone very, very special. I couldn't believe the music I was listening to. I'd honestly never heard anything quite like it in my life.

The first time I met the man was not long in coming. A couple of days later, I arrived at work at Country Cousin in the evening to find a very tearful friend. There'd been a row. I was listening to and consoling my friend at the top of the stairs leading from the street when the door at the front of the staircase burst open. My friend turned and yelled down to someone whom at first I couldn't see .

"Don't you *dare* come up here ! This is *my* sanctuary. These are *my* friends!" My friend then disappeared.

Gingerly I looked down the stairs just as this amazingly flamboyant and almost incredible figure decided to storm the steep. Freddie almost flew up the stairs, furious and in a lather of anger. However, when he realised that our friend had left, he calmed down. I asked him if he'd like a drink. He refused. In those days he hardly drank at all.

He sat down at the bar and I sat with him whilst Christopher Hunter busied himself with the restaurant's opening preparations. Freddie was completely open and utterly honest from the start.

"You're a good friend of his," he said, not particularly bothering to lower his voice. "He's very difficult, you know. You'll have to come and help me find him". He was quite insistent. So was Christopher Hunter.

"She *is* employed to run a restaurant, you know!" came a voice from the other end of the bar.

Nevertheless, off we went and that was how I first got to know Freddie, cruising the streets of London in a boat-like limousine as he searched for our mutual friend to patch up their quarrel.

ELAINE PAIGE

My first impressions of Freddie was that he was always larger than life. He projected enormous energy and tremendous enthusiasm in everything he did and I was in complete awe of him. Away from the spotlight and all the glamour, I discovered he could be so down to earth, sensitive and thoughtful. It was very much like seeing both sides of a coin; one moment he appeared to be completely over the top and the next he was this really 'regular kind of guy'.

JAMES ARTHURS

I guess it was late 1975. John Reid had just taken over as *Queen*'s manager and Peter Straker and I went together to the Christmas Eve concert at Hammersmith Odeon. A week later, Freddie came with Mary Austin to Straker's then regular New Year's Eve party. That's when we first met.

I seem to remember Freddie spent most of the time sequestered in the kitchen. He was a little shy, to some extent, rather than aloof. I was mostly in the front room and wound up chatting with Mary for quite a while. Freddie would occasionally come in to see that Mary was OK and eventually he and I wound up talking too. We found we had a couple of interests in common - we were both Japanophiles and we both loved antiques.

I was living just outside New York at that time but I returned to London every Christmas to spend a week with my family who all made the pilgrimage to London for the annual reunion. Freddie suggested he and I get together to do a little antique shopping next time he was in New York and so a few months later he called me and off we went on a buying spree and that was really when our friendship started.

PETER FREESTONE

I met Freddie both through opera and at The Royal Opera House in Covent Garden, London. I'd fallen in love with opera at the age of eighteen when I saw my first, Il Trovatore with, ironically, Montserrat Caballé. However, it was to be four and half years before I was to meet the man who would ultimately re-introduce me to my first diva.

I was born in St. Helier's Hospital in Carshalton in 1955 and for the first five years of my life, with my mother, my father and my elder brother, lived in Mitcham. My mother had been a nurse and my father had been in the army. When I was six, the family moved to India. Although my mother had coincidentally, nursed in Poona very near where Freddie had been at school, it was into the hotel business that they moved. They ran a small hotel in Calcutta for some five years. As far as our schooling was concerned, it was to boarding school in Ootacamund in Southern India that my brother and I were sent, the same kind of school which Freddie was sent to from a similarly great distance, where Latin and the classics were taught as a matter of course along the lines of preparatory and public school education in the 'mother' country. My brother and I, only thirteen and six respectively, were a long way from our parents and we travelled the hundreds of miles south from Calcutta by steam train and only spent a couple of months with our family in Calcutta as during the hotter vacations, we met my mother and father at Conoor in the hills away from the searing heat.

We returned to England when I was eleven and we lived in that part of London bounded by Westbourne Grove and Notting Hill Gate. I've always lived in West London apart from a very brief twelve month sojourn in Tufnell Park. I'm not boasting when I say that I was a very bright child but because I had missed the eleven plus examination and was therefore outside 'the system', I was sent to the Isaac Newton Secondary Modern School in North Kensington where I learned precisely nothing. I'd learned all that Isaac Newton could teach me back in India.

However, I came out with the requisite nine 'O' levels although their attempt to inculcate a whole 'A' level course in three subjects in a year failed dismally and I left at eighteen.

Whilst at school, I had worked at weekends at Selfridges in Oxford Street and so I took up their offer of a place on a catering management course which had been effectively built around me and by the time I was nineteen, I was the youngest assistant manager that the store had ever had. It was also where, again coincidentally, I was to meet the young Jim Hutton for the first time although it was to be several years before we were to meet again and then, as you know, under very different circumstances.

I must be giving the impression that I was work crazy because also at that time, when I was twenty, I started working as a part-time dresser for opera at the Royal Opera House after working at Selfridges all day. I might have been tired but at least I got the chance to hear a huge amount of opera even if it was whilst waiting in the wings with changes of costume and props.

In 1977, when I was twenty two and after leaving Selfridges, I went to work full time for the Royal Opera House Wardrobe department as I had also started to act as dresser for the company of the Royal Ballet.

It must have been either September or October 1979 when I met Freddie for the first time. It was the days of the Gala - The Pre-Aids Galas. Almost every Sunday, part of the Royal Ballet or the company of the Royal Opera House would give a charity performance and there was usually, probably always, a mystery guest.

The costumes for this particular gala, specifically a ballet one, were being designed by Ian Spurling and I think it must have been Wayne Eagling who was in charge of finding the mystery guest. It was of course Freddie as we were all delighted to find out when he came in to the wardrobe department to finalise his costume. The clothes he was to wear were his own but we had to make sure that they were going to work with the other costumes.

Apart from that he was much smaller than I had thought him to be from having occasionally caught the band and their videos on television, it was a very different Mr. Mercury to the one I had seen taking polite sips with Mary in the tea room at the Derry and Toms Biba way back in 1973, which had been my first and only sighting of him. Those were the days of all the hair and that wretched fox fur jacket with the too-short sleeves which has been chronicled to death. It was also a very different Mr. Mercury to the one that I occasionally saw in full flight whilst on *Queen* performances or, heaven for fend, at home!

He arrived with only Paul Prenter, not the entourage he was often associated with and it was obvious that he was in a milieu which he found, well ... intimidating is perhaps too strong but it was a circumstance with which he wasn't familiar and Freddie could be very shy, seemingly deferential in areas where he wasn't one hundred percent sure. But he was definitely excited at the prospect of appearing with the Royal Ballet.

Although in the performance, Freddie mimed to a backing track, when the company broke ranks on-stage to reveal him standing there in black leather jacket and silver sequined body stocking, it was the first public performance of *Crazy Little Thing Called Love* which he sang as well as *Bohemian Rhapsody* as he was being manhandled (should I say physically choreographed?) by the company. After having worked with ballet dancers, he felt rather clumsy when approaching the little balletic steps he had been using in his stage act until then. He came away from that gala with a great respect for the real thing.

Of course as soon as the dancers parted and there he was, everyone in the audience knew it was Freddie Mercury. The audience loved it and, strangely, it was the only one of those galas I ever saw from the front as I had bought my seat in anticipation. Freddie stole and closed the show.

Afterwards, the party moved to Legends club in Old Burlington Street and I found myself to talking a great deal to Paul Prenter. However, when I wended my way home at the end of the evening, I had absolutely no idea that I would ever be seeing Freddie again."

Those were the days of our lives

PART II

CAUGHT IN THE LANDSLIDE

DERRICK BRANCHE

St. Peter's school, Panchgani afforded all who went there a very special time. It was the best place I can think of for a kid to go to school. We were given enormous freedom, support and encouragement and the school was exceptionally well-run. I can think of nothing ugly about the place or the time we had there.

I was a pupil at St. Peter's between the ages of ten and fifteen. I can't remember if Faroukh, or Freddie as we would alternatively call him, returned to St. Peter's after my last term or not. He went back to Africa as usual for the holidays and I went to England as my mother, since the death of my father, wanted for her own reasons to get me away from India. However, five years' school companionship is a long time and, in my opinion, one of the most formative times of anyone's life and although he's not here to refute it, I recall that Freddie's and my school days were, if not the proverbially happiest days of our lives, then certainly a time of great joy, for in our innocence we had a marvellous time.

St. Peter's was run exactly on the lines of an English public school. The routine of the school's life and the content of our education would have been replicated exactly at Haileybury or Rugby. St. Peter's was a Church of England school and everyone underwent that regime whether their families were of Christian, Hindu, Muslim or, as in Freddie's case, the Parsee faith. The only difference in the school schedule was that St. Peter's celebrated every Indian holiday too. They were very ecumenical circumstances and the tolerance and acceptance that was bred there was actively encouraged by the school authorities. The Christian angle was never overplayed in any missionary way although I cannot deny that our upbringing at St. Peter's had more to do with the Victorian than the new Elizabethan age. As far as Freddie was concerned, this traditionalism, I think, was a positive advantage for amongst the regular academicism, there was of course a school choir which sang all the traditional choral works and hymns and which practised regularly in order to lead the singing at the school's church services. The choir was about twenty five strong and we would often be mixed with girls from one of our sister schools in the town. Not only did Freddie love the choir but I believe he also loved one of the girls too, fifteen year old Gita Bharucha if I'm not greatly mistaken!

That first day we arrived at St. Peter's, we all filed into the school and then found our way to our dormitory which had about twenty beds in it. We five, myself, Freddie, Bruce, Farang and Victory found ourselves beds next to each other and we were to remain as a company throughout our career at St. Peter's.

As we grew older, we had the chance of a dormitory to ourselves and – whether or not this proximity had anything to do with it I have no idea – we took the room for we had formed ourselves into the school rock band. We had become *The Hectics* and it was as the piano player in *The Hectics* that Freddie first performed as a musician, cranking out a mean boogie woogie even at that tender age.

As I have indicated, the school was very free with encouragement and *The Hectics* suddenly seemed to have taken over the music room where we practised. We would play at school concerts, at the school's annual fête and at other such times when the girls from the neighbouring schools would come along and stand in front and scream, just like they had obviously heard that girls the world over were beginning to do when faced with current idols such as Cliff Richard or Elvis Presley, Little Richard and Fats Domino, these latter two being Freddie's and my particular favourites.

Strange though it might be to report, in those days, Freddie was quite content to stay well in the background as Bruce Murray slipped easily into the role of lead singer. In fact, Freddie didn't seem a natural front man at all. It should go without saying that it amazed me watching him become such an enormous star. The person whom I knew as Freddie Bulsara at school would never have been able to achieve so much, so consummately. Although I remember his shyness – and he was very reticent – there was a side to him which was always somewhat frenzied. Although he wasn't at all loud by nature or character, he was known on occasion to shed his prim demeanour. I can hear him now screeching like a banshee as he rushed down the dormitory screaming: "Who's pinched my *soap*!!" He'd even scream at the teachers if accused of something he either hadn't done or felt he should vehemently deny... "No I *didn't* do it!!"

He was no shrinking violet. As enterprising as children are at boarding schools, we were no different and Freddie would immediately join in the schemes. We would go on 'tuck raids' undertaken before such luxury rations were locked away by the housemistresses and matrons. Freddie would always be the one keeping watch and may I say he made a very efficient lookout.

There were only fifteen of us in our class. Branche came just before Bulsara in the register of names and we were close all through our school careers. I always wanted to be an actor. I don't know what Freddie wanted to be although he was always very good at art. We were all fond of music and in addition to our efforts as members of *The Hectics*, our musical education was greatly widened by Mr. Davis, a teacher who would play us recordings of other sorts of music. I remember Freddie loving the operas which Mr. Davis played us and in addition, we used to listen avidly to recordings of Olivier, Gielgud and other Old Vic actors in Shakespeare's plays. The time Mr. Davis set aside for these sessions was in the evening, after tea and before we went in to prep. I can remember us sitting enraptured, enthralled at these recordings of the great English classics.

Mr. Rowe, our housemaster, who was also the English master, would produce and direct the statutory school plays where any girls' roles would often be fulfilled in true Shakespearean tradition by other boys. I hasten to add I can't remember Freddie ever being cast as a girl despite his later appearance in his own *Great Pretender* video as the manic housewife with the vacuum cleaner. However, I can remember a production of a play called oddly *Cure For The Fidgets* in which I played the fidget dressed in a mac for some reason whilst Freddie, I believe, played the doctor curing the said fidgets, dressed immaculately in a suit, heavy spectacles and his hair swept back almost in a quiff. In another play, Freddie was bending over during the course of a performance and the schoolboy actor standing behind him accidentally poked him in the backside with the tip of a sword. Freddie was outraged. He sprang upright, spun round, broke character and screeched at his astonished fellow thespian:

"There was no need to do *that!!*"

He slapped the poor boy across the face and rushed off the stage, refusing to return until he had received medical attention from Matron Thompson.

Needless to say the photographs of these productions record the now-famous hands flapping wildly. Those hands were never still, always being waved around with high intensity to emphasise whatever point he was making at the time. Whenever I think of him, I always remember him smiling. He seemed to be perpetually smiling and thinking of that makes me smile too, especially as I recall him taking part in the school's sports day races. He wasn't at all fond of games but participated as we all did. Seeing Freddie, scurrying down the track like an even more demented version of Jerry Lewis, hands flapping and legs going every which way but the way they were supposed to, is a joy to remember.

DAVID MINNS

Freddie must have seen how close, loyal and discreet my group of friends were to one another; Me, David Evans, Peter Straker, Eddie Howell, Clodagh Wallace, Sarah Harrison, Suzanne Bertish and many countless others formed a support network for each others' lives and careers. I think Freddie must have felt very comfortable being amongst that group of people with such diverse backgrounds, talents and directions. For the first time, he could be himself both in public and in private but being able to do so had its emotional cost.

I know he was tormented by some form of guilt that he had about his past life and that included both his family and, of course, Mary. He went to great lengths to protect them from his public life and image and at times his private life as well. I was very aware of these efforts and felt deeply for him as he tried to make some sense of his behaviour. He rarely discussed his family with anyone.

Relationships are notoriously difficult things and it is doubly difficult to attempt a relationship with a famous person and virtually impossible with someone like Freddie. I think he really wanted a variety of separate people surrounding him to perform the various support roles which are usually combined in a single partner. Our friendship was based on a mutual love of music, eating in good restaurants not to mention our appreciation of all forms of art and antiques.

I remember not long after him extravagantly purchasing a Silver Shadow Rolls Royce from Jack Barclay in Berkeley Square, we were in the car approaching Sotheby's in Bond Street and I mentioned that as he loved them so much why didn't he start to get seriously interested in buying some Japanese woodcuts. At the time, they were his passion. I meant that he should start to become a collector, investing his money in what he loved.

He was less than complimentary about my suggestion and I seem to remember getting out of the car at the next set of lights after a very heated discussion about money!

"What!" he screamed, "I couldn't *possibly* afford anything from a place like Sotheby's!"

He really thought of himself as not being in that league although it was not long before the word ' afford' was stricken from his vocabulary.

I decided to buy a catalogue for the sale at Sotheby's. We went along to the sale, and all in all, he bought about thirty woodcuts, spending well over £20,000. Strange how a pauper one moment can in the space of a few short weeks suddenly see himself as a rival to John Paul Getty!

He never looked back after attending that first sale and continued, I understand, to plan the expansion of his collection until the week he died. I feel very proud that I gave him that first impetus to begin to

CAUGHT IN THE LANDSLIDE

amass what must now be an outstanding collection of art and antiques. I must say that in many ways I think he preferred his collection of objects to his collection of people. It gave him an escape from the world of rock music, which was, of course, his other great passion.

That passion went very deep. We would often be sitting at home when Freddie would become progressively very restless and fidgety. He was the most terrible fidget. He always *had* to be doing something. Every waking moment. His mind was occupied with schemes, with lyrics and plans which would often become obsessive to the point of his becoming completely and angrily frustrated. At this time, he was very keen on hearing the opinions of others and would endlessly ask me what I thought of this or that lyric, always paying a compliment for what he thought of as a constructive suggestion. It was fascinating to watch how he would soak up every atom of life, every particle of every person and situation he encountered to assist in the creative process of his songwriting.

To me and to many others, he was a consummate songwriter. Not many people realised either what an excellent and innovative pianist he was; Rachmaninoff he wasn't, but in terms of the way he used the piano for composition, he was unrivalled.

I also hadn't quite realised how much Freddie drew from his relationships the ideas he needed for his work. He wrote many songs about the people he loved, not to mention songs about those of whom he wasn't quite so fond! For example, I would often accuse him of holding deeply old fashioned opinions. Perhaps it was this which inspired him to write *Good Old Fashioned Lover Boy*?

I still maintain he *was* old fashioned. Amongst his other eccentricities, Freddie in those days was a great letter writer. I have boxes of letters from him, from wherever he found himself in the world; where most people would be content merely to 'phone, Freddie would write as well. I understood that later in his life, he sadly stopped being so old fashioned.

One song I remember him writing specifically is on the *Day at the Races* album. Before recording it, he played it to me and I remember feeling shattered for days that anyone was prepared to write a song like that for me for that it is what he told me the lyrics were about. It was a worthwhile vindication for at the time, our friendship was under severe pressure from many quarters. It was ironic that later on in his career, I knew exactly about whom he had written subsequent songs. He was awfully clever like that.

Freddie's world was all-consuming and it wasn't long before my whole life was completely devoted to his existence. In retrospect, although this turned out to be a big mistake for both of us, there was no other way for our friendship to be sustained.

Freddie had formed several companies for music publishing and music production. One of the first projects undertaken by him via these companies was the production of my client Eddie Howell's single *Man from Manhattan* for Warner Brothers. Freddie persuaded Brian May to play on the track and Freddie himself, of course, layered a few harmonies as well as contributing by caressing the ivories. *Queen* played *Man from Manhattan* at soundchecks during the 1976 world tour. I think it was a welcome relief from their own material.

Being a workaholic, Freddie then decided he was going to produce an album for our close friend Peter Straker. Freddie was envious of very little in life. If he ever was, he kept very quiet about it but one thing he envied most and unashamedly of all was Peter's voice and, as he was patently not going to come by the voice for his own use, the next best thing was to own it. Recording Straker's first album was a very happy experience for us all and Goose Productions soon signed the album to EMI. Freddie entered into the recordings with as high a degree of perfectionism and discipline that he would have applied to a *Queen* album although it has to be said that Freddie wanted more than anything to do something for his friend.

This generosity of Freddie's has become legendary although the recipients of it were often perplexed exactly as to why they had been singled out. He didn't need an occasion to give someone a present; any excuse would do. To look back, it seems sad that in return he received so little from the many beneficiaries of his bounty. In reverse, when he did receive gifts, he was often openly suspicious of their validity. Freddie wanted everything to be original or at least rare. A minor example of this trait was when he received a gold disc for *A Night At The Opera* from his record company EMI. He was unconvinced that the record beneath the glass was his own. After he had prised the frame open "sorry, it accidentally broke itself, Sir Joseph, may we have another one? Freddie insisted I played it; he was deeply impressed and somewhat taken aback that it was indeed a copy of *A Night At The Opera*. He never again accused EMI of being cheapskates.

His increasing financial good fortune also gave Freddie the opportunity to indulge in another favourite extravagance which was throwing parties. Birthday celebrations were treated with particularly detailed attention. The birthday party in question was, after all, a Freddie Mercury Production!

The one I'd like to recall in some detail was the famous thirtieth birthday party bash in 1977 held at the notorious cabaret club Country Cousin run by Christopher Hunter and our dear friend Cherry Brown.

Freddie insisted that I throw the party for him and make all the arrangements. His single material contribution apart from settling the huge final bill was his week long project of writing by hand every single one of the hundred and fifty invitations. The thought of having them printed was overridden by his original whimsical and charming insistence on writing each one personally although it didn't occurred to him how long this exercise would take. The guest list who had been exhorted to 'dress to kill', included Elton John, John Reid, Tim Curry, Divine, Kenny Everett, Ken and Dolly East, Jim and Claudia Beach and every luminary in London's music business.

Apart from a very lavish banquet which comprised everything from oysters to lobsters, game to sausages, caviar to kumquats all displayed in table centrepieces which looked like cornucopia, I and Pete Brown, their tour manager, had arranged for the evening's entertainment a cast of conjurors, acrobats, a snake charming stripper and some very rude and clothes-less girls. Divine managed to spray a whole magnum of Cristal champagne between the legs of one of the dancers who took the compliment lying down.

The most expensive item on that evening's bill was the flowers. Freddie adored flowers. Christopher Hunter returned from Covent Garden early that morning with about thirty boxes of blooms - irises, lilies, orchids, freesia, gladioli, roses – every flower imaginable which was available at that time of year. These decorated the tables, the pillars, the walls, the bar area and the loos. The whole effect was spectacular and as his first big party, Freddie's thirtieth birthday celebration opened the floodgates to what became a tide of lavish and remarkable parties which marked the course of the rest of his life.

However, in those early days of his success, there was also an incredible sense of innocence about him, verging at times on social naivety. I often felt that I was his teacher and his prop, a buttress in social situations. He was very nervous with strangers, people he didn't know well but when he relaxed into company he was incredibly entertaining and indeed an interesting man with great knowledge and awareness.

His high standards and insistence on perfectionism as well as having his own way often marred his own enjoyment.

During the 1976 American tour of *A Night At The Opera* for example, after every date they played, a party was thrown by either the local concert promoter or the record company, for *Queen* were still relatively unknown in the USA and it was essential that the band be seen at these functions, especially the lead singer. More often than not, Freddie would take one look at the assembled media bigwigs and industry minions only to turn on his heel and flounce out. My point is that at his own parties he felt himself in control. At parties thrown for him but not by him, he felt detached and uncomfortable and his underlying shyness and lack of confidence welled up to cause some of the most explosive tantrums he was known for.

These tantrums were only ever wreaked upon those who had no recourse against his ill-will. He disliked being contradicted and that he could be wrong about anything was a thought which never entered his mind. With those few, notably his fellow *Queen* members, who stood up to him, his display of backing down when clearly he was wrong was akin to that of a scorned and defeated peacock retreating in short trousers, bravely clutching his tuck-box.

Indeed, it was this very vulnerability that made him both so endearing and yet formidable for it is vulnerability which has everything to do with confidence and it is the question of his confidence which has to be mentioned for it was an important part of Freddie's persona.

Although he was the master at visually presenting himself as the vampire of glitter rock, this underlying insecurity spilled over into his offstage self-image. He knew how important it was to maintain his levels of self-confidence and he knew how to compensate for his lack of them. He knew his weaknesses only too well and equally knew how to avoid them as in the example I've given in the party situation. Like John McEnroe, Freddie would become abusive and angry to pump himself up in order to conquer those situations into which protocol or mere necessity had forced him against his wishes.

When *Queen* appeared in the Hyde Park Concert in 1976, the band left John Reid's house in Montpellier Square in a laundry van and were driven in secret to the VIP area where we all hopped out ready for their appearance. Freddie had been in a very good mood but as soon as he saw the hundreds of invited and uninvited backstage guests, he became incensed and yelled at them as they gawped at him:

"You f...ing load of wankers! Go out and watch it with the rest of them!"

He was gladiatorial in that sense. He had to pit himself against an imaginary foe in order to get his adrenaline going before facing the music.

Although Freddie loved to perform and was phenomenal at doing so and went to great lengths to visually please his paying audience, he hated being an object of scrutiny away from the limelight. During a shopping expedition at Christmas 1976 in Harrods, not conspicuously dressed as Freddie Mercury, star, we were walking through the silverware department when a group of schoolgirls spotted him and as soon as the screams rang out, Freddie made a quick sprint for the nearest exit followed by his driver, Derek Balcombe, leaving me to fend off the pursuing posse of gymslips. However, for the time being although he disliked the invasive attention of his admirers, nothing was going to stop him leading as public a private life as he wanted. I even remember catching a bus with him once when a cab couldn't be found in the street. The faces of fellow passengers were a treat to behold. I think the shock value thrilled him. He liked to reveal himself but he hated being revealed.

After nearly three years and experiencing both the international rise of *Queen* to pre-eminence and seeing Freddie in turn becoming the mega-star, many new faces began to appear at the gates of Freddie's kingdom. Most were invited but only some remained. The transient visitors I could put up with but those who where obviously there to stay made my state of mind intolerable and my position untenable and

I found that my decision to get out had been almost made for me. I decided that out was better than in. Although we had obviously drifted apart, it did not seem to be a situation which caused Freddie too much concern although when I made it clear that I wanted to put an end to our association, to my amazement Freddie displayed utter disbelief.

Of course, he could not understand and could see no reason why our friendship should not continue. However, one of the few things that Freddie was not good at was being a good liar. He was hopeless. Realising this, rather than lie to himself, he merely distorted reality to make himself believe he was doing nothing blameworthy. But then, don't we all?

To do him full justice, he was deeply shocked to find that with the help of my neighbour Sarah Forbes, I ultimately left the flat in London and went to stay with my friends David and Edmund in Somerset.

When I returned to London, Freddie did everything he could to try and make amends but I had made a decision and for better or worse, for it affected my whole existence, I wanted to free myself of the anguish which being part of his world had caused both me and others around us.

Although we were in contact for about a year afterwards, I seldom saw him for many years as he was living mainly in New York and Munich. Out of the blue, I got a call to come to the famous Hat Party at Logan Place on his fortieth birthday. Then, after the death of my friend Janet O'Hanlon whom I had been nursing and after Peter Straker had come to lodge with me, my friendship with Freddie was to some extend resumed.

He invited me to a studio where he and Mike Moran were recording an album with Montserrat Caballé and I arrived only to see my former friend displaying the discoloured areas on his face which were the outward manifestations of one of the Aids-related illnesses which we now understand were beginning to affect him. We exchanged huge hugs. He realised that I had been taken aback by his appearance and exclaimed:

"It's alright, dear! There's no need to look at me like that. I've just been drinking too much vodka and doing too much... The doctors say I have a liver complaint."

Oh, God, I thought.

DAVID EVANS

Incredible although this may sound, it is often hard, being so unfamous oneself, to have famous friends. I'm blessed with many friends, thank God, some of whom are famous and some who aren't and those of them who are will I trust forgive me when I say that I'm not sure I want them to be any more famous than they already are because I'm not sure I could cope.

I knew I had to stand back from Freddie, keep a respectful distance. Life around him after *Bohemian Rhapsody* had taken on a November 5th quality. Many of those who knew him, who were involved with him, had seen the blue touch paper of his particular firework being lit and, obeying the instructions on the box, we had retired safely. Others were caught in the blast, spectacular though it was, of his ascent to the dizzying heights of international fame. There was a volcanic, pent-up urgency about the quality of Freddie's ambition and I refer not only to his professional goals but to his private ones.

Though I may have taken my propensity for worrying about other people too far in my life, I have never been able to manipulate my perspectives to exclude them. To be specific, I was very aware of what Mary Austin was being put through because of Freddie's insistence on pursuing his friendship with my flatmate David to its ultimate limit. As I had thought, Freddie and David needed their own space and it wasn't one which included Mary. Mary had proved and was to prove over time, one of the enduring foundations which supported not only Freddie Mercury, star but also Freddie Mercury, man. The two incarnations were *very* different, by the way. I had to withdraw from being too close to Freddie for to have remained in proximity would have courted disaster for our friendship. I would have had to comment, to criticise and to censure. I didn't because I knew I didn't have to. Freddie knew what was happening only too well.

By this time, David had moved out of the flat in Putney, Freddie had moved from 100 Holland Road, he to Stafford Terrace and Mary to her own flat and I had spent a fateful summer in Scotland, in the summer of 1976.

In Edinburgh, my boss John Reid, prompted by an inspiration from the late and sadly missed David Bell, then of Scottish Television, had sponsored the launch of The Playhouse Theatre as a major rock venue. In my naive enthusiasm, I had encouraged and supported the venture. Naive? Yes. I had never run a theatre and certainly could not have envisaged the stress and problems that being responsible for opening one could have entailed. Needless to say all John's acts played the venue – Elton, *Queen*, Kiki, Kevin Ayers... Whether it was sheer fatigue, disillusionment with the music business, disappointment as to the behaviour of several of my illustrious associates, I can't say after such a long time but whatever the combination of factors, I decided to jack in my career, such as it was. "Yes, John... I quit!"

I had met Edmund Murray in Edinburgh and I had decided to remain in Scotland; I saw Freddie less often than before but always when Ed and I came to London. I felt strange about it, seeing Freddie from the point of view of my new, non-musical life. His world had swallowed up mine completely. David was now not only working with Freddie on a daily basis but my old friend and former client Peter Straker was being produced as a recording artist by Freddie and was signed to Freddie's Goose Productions recording company. My ex-secretary Alex Foster had taken over my job at John Reid's and was now dealing with Freddie and *Queen* on an everyday level. I didn't feel resentful, I merely marvelled at how attractive my world must have been and was certainly perplexed for a time at my own actions for abandoning it with such relief, for I did feel relieved to be no longer a part of it.

Edmund and I moved down to Bath. Freddie, always curious, came down to see the place which was a wonderful small country house in acres of grounds. I think he was curious as to what it might be like to own a mini-estate. He saw what tremendously hard work it was and never owned anything with any more garden than was absolutely necessary.

The break-up with his relationship with David was not long in coming. The pressures of Freddie's stardom, his schedule, his presti-digitation act regarding his past, current and future lives had proved too much, I feel, for both of them and Freddie, I think, felt that he could not give any more than he was already giving without compromising and Freddie *never* compromised. Neither did he brook rejection or defeat with equanimity. The heat was being turned up full. I remember the instance of an Art Deco chinoiserie cocktail cabinet I had bought in Scotland and which I admitted to Freddie was for sale. I announced how much I wanted for it. Freddie offered for it, via David; I declined and counter-offered; he re-offered and upon my decline, none of us spoke to each other for months. There must have been hundreds of other instances with many, many people but one of the traits of his stardom was beginning to emerge. In order to survive and persevere, in order to maintain the momentum he and his career had now attracted, Freddie found it difficult to have people around him who were difficult. It happens around stars; some call it sycophancy, some call it arse-licking. Its actually called making life easier both for the star and the satellite and perhaps its not just with stars; perhaps it happens to an extent in lots of outwardly devoted friendships.

But, whatever the reasons, the process begins to warp the perspectives of both the star and the satellite. Both sides seem to end up wanting more than the other wants to give. And the star seems to glitter further and further away, one step-removed. There comes the time when, to see your star, you have to get through the asteroid belt. Thankfully, that never happened to me for it would have killed any friendship but it started to happen, nevertheless and, I fancy, was prerequisite to Freddie's life becoming removed from the reality which involves the everyday problems which keep us all, however individualistic and special and heady we think of ourselves, with feet vaguely touching the floor. Cut off and removed and insulated from the world of cares, why not as Richard O'Brien puts it in the Rocky Horror Show: "Give yourself over to absolute pleasure..."

In my introduction, I referred to Freddie being a late-starter and in the way of pursuing his sexuality, I think he was. The years I didn't see him much, between 1979 and 1984 were those he found himself being led by several different drummers and the rhythm they set and the directions they led were very much at odds with the initial transition he had made between his two sexual orientations. It was obvious that Freddie was not satisfied with cosy domestic arrangements with any sex.

I didn't know the Freddie who rampaged through those years at all, but from what I have been told, his life in Munich and in New York seems to have been hectic, late-night and greedy. His thirties were not unlike many other people's thirties in the western world and certainly not in the western world's metropolis.

The legacy of the brief few years of sexual liberation, especially for homosexual people was a greedy, often insatiable appetite for anything and everything new; people, experiences and places. I understand it completely. Years, nay, centuries of repression and suppression had produced a volcanic and post-eruptive headlong desire to slake the rampant appetites of fantasy by creating and then indulging in a carnal and venal reality which it was thought along with drugs and even strange new religions would help achieve fulfilment. I think every generation has seen something of the same. When Cole Porter wrote *Anything Goes*, there was something of the same acknowledgement of abandonment underpinning his observation.

Freddie certainly saw what was available, knew he could have whatever he wanted and went for it. Sadly, like so many of us, he paid the ultimate price.

He must have known for years that he was ill. Although I saw him occasionally, it was only three or four years after I met Nigel with whom I now live, that I felt I wanted to expose us to Freddie's world. Though I would see, and looked forward to seeing, Freddie on my own, I didn't feel at all safe in exposing Nigel to what I had intuited was a rather wild and heady society. I obviously *have* been too much aware of what I *thought* were other people's feelings because we all met up at Freddie's fortieth birthday party and, of course, everyone got on like a house on fire although the Freddie who was forty, was quieter, almost reticent compared to the one I had encountered in the wild years.

I liked this later Freddie a lot. He was very much like he'd been when I'd first known him. As the years wore on and he became more and more worn down by the illness which accompanied his Aids condition, he became almost solicitous in our relationship. He would ask how people were, remember incidents and occasions I supposed would have been long forgotten. We had lunch, we visited, we gossiped and chattered... We gave up smoking at the same time and then, drinking. Latterly, it was obvious he was ill but he didn't want to discuss it. That he didn't want to talk about it bothered me not a jot. I'd encountered the same situation with another friend, Colin Higgins, a director and writer in Hollywood, who had had to face the same terminal situation and who took the same course of decisions: Say nothing and if confronted, deny everything.

Unless you are asked into someone's innermost world of problems, unless the door be opened, however small the opening might be, it is very difficult to enter, doubly difficult when your friend happens to be, as Tony King once so aptly put it, "The Greta Garbo of rock 'n' roll."

There came a time when it was impossible for me not to guess. Freddie must have sensed this for he rang me and asked to come to lunch, just the two of us. To say I was honoured to be taken into his confidence is not enough. As an act of friendship, such an exchange of confidence is unsurpassed. There have been too many in my life recently not to know that I am humbled every time. There is nothing anyone can do... But I fancy that if you are ill, just knowing that there are people you can call on any time you want to is at least a comforting diversion, faced though you are with what must be the seemingly insuperable task of being made to let go.

EDDIE HOWELL

I don't really remember how or when Freddie offered his services as producer for *Man From Manhattan*. A deal of interest had been engendered even by the simple revox demo I had made of the song which had not been included on the *Eddie Howell Gramophone Record.*

At Werter Road, David Minns' flat in Putney, Freddie too heard the demo and he too loved the song. At that point he wanted to be involved in some way and it was soon after that that I was told he wanted to produce the track. Warners were delighted and we had a carte blanche situation as far as budget was concerned, an early eye opener as to the sycophantic reactions of the record industry to its current icons. Strangely, Freddie treated most industry minions cursed with sycophancy with appropriate oversight and didn't seem to take any notice of fawning whatever.

Privately, before the sessions were booked, I went round to Freddie's flat at 100 Holland Road which was dominated even in its Victorian splendour by a huge grand piano. Freddie had been working meticulously on the harmonies and with the ultimate benefit of my presence began writing them down on manuscript paper for the session. He was nothing if not thorough. The work was not crocheted and quavered but the chord symbols were all in place as would be expected. However, the melody line snaked like a graph over the stave, note by note, and I was fascinated to watch as Freddie followed the ups and downs of the notes with the accompanying words or syllables of words which comprised the harmonies, a sort of uphill, downhill writing which I had seen neither before nor since. It was just his way of doing what he saw as his job and it proved to me that he was instinctively totally at one with the feeling of my song.

Suddenly, we're in Sarm East Studios and we've booked musicians. The sessions would begin around twelve and I was staying in Clapham, which I had rented from Jackie Krost, Barry Krost's younger brother. Derek Balcombe with Freddie and David in the back would pick me up in Freddie's Daimler limo to take me to Whitechapel. Freddie would have his tape recorder brimming over with ideas for the forthcoming session for which the crème de la crème of current London session men had been hired. Barry de Souza on drums, American Jerome Rimson on bass, Freddie on piano and me on acoustic guitar as well as Brian May on lead guitar. Roger Taylor wasn't included as Freddie thought it would make the whole thing too Queeny.

Freddie's un-flagging enthusiasm kept everyone afloat single-handed. I remember the reaction of our seasoned session men to his powers of motivation for I have a sneaking feeling that they were expecting more of a campy dilettante behind the desk rather than the consummate professional he always was. In fact, it was the first time I noticed how Freddie made people cross barriers they might otherwise have sneered at. Even my very masculine brother Terry enthused over the heroic and outrageous flamboyance of Freddie's personality. Despite all the strutting and the fretting, millions of people found that Freddie in some way brought out their alter egos, the person they would all like to have been for a time, if only for a time...

Immediate memory forces me to recall that the most integral part of these sessions were not the mixing desk or the mikes but Freddie's hairbrush and his comb. They became a permanent fixture on the sound desk as photographers like Mick Rock were in those days constantly tripping in and out to record the boy for posterity. In those days, being photographed was not a problem.

The final note of the recorded version of *Man From Manhattan* sounds from a bell. Freddie insisted on this even though I thought it relatively unimportant. Even in those days, studio time was £60 an hour and I was consequently astonished at Freddie's stubborn determination to include this bell on the track. Barry de Souza was delegated to play the bell which he duly did. However, to achieve the correct whirling sound that Freddie wanted, it was found that the bell had to be spun and so, twirling Barry de Souza ultimately twirled his bell to Freddie's satisfaction. It took an hour, I'm here to say but at the end of the hour, nothing could be recorded as Freddie found that the pre-pitched bell was in the wrong key. Panic! Freddie rushed out to his beloved piano to establish which key the bell *should* be pitched in and horror, upon horrors, 'D' was the correct note and there wasn't a 'D' pitched bell in the studio. Someone was duly despatched to scour the music hire shops of London. I learned the true meaning of the word go-fer that day for six or seven hours later when the go-fer returned, having clocked up an extra £400 of studio time, everyone found that they had been too utterly exhausted waiting for the bell and so Freddie extravagantly and with no apparent concern for the rising costs of this single note, ordered the evacuation to his favourite Indian restaurant for dinner which was the second most important feature of Freddie's sessions. The poor bell was the un-rung victim of the hour and I had learned a major lesson in record showmanship which is that perfection doesn't come cheap.

Freddie also made the whole thing fun. The prima donna aspect of his personality was part of his method of motivation under studio circumstances and enabled him to get exactly what he wanted. But I remember laughing a lot and feeling fairly frivolous as the adrenaline pumped round at fever pitch. He said to me:

"You should sue Warner Brothers, dear, if this isn't a hit."

I know he really cared about that week's sessions and quite enjoyed being the back-room boy for once. Any unnecessary glamour was banished entirely for the sake of a job well-done. Although I never felt comfortable with him, I knew he was zoning in to my particular way of expressing myself and was doing everything he could not to force his own personality either on my session or my song. Although he was on the crest of his own wave, I feel that he got something out of the experience too.

PETER STRAKER

A friendship which lasts sixteen years is a hell of a long time. It's a tough one. What *do* I think?

It was hard to avoid Freddie at first as both our paths were constantly crossing. We both ate in the same restaurants, drank at the same clubs and knew the same people. In the nineteen thirties, they would have had a name for our loose group, like the Algonquin Round Table or the Scott and Zelda Fitzgerald set. Business people, artists of every shape and medium. Painters, actors and actresses, media folk, musicians, dancers both classical and modern. It was a pot pourri, a heady combination, something which I'm sure still exists but which to me remains rather special and unique within my memory. It was inevitable that Freddie and I would get to know each other more than just two ships which pass in the night.

It was in November 1975, at one of my several birthday parties, this one a fancy dress affair at Hurlingham Road to which I invited Freddie. The theme was 'Come As Your Favourite Person'. Freddie said he *might* come but that he wouldn't be in fancy dress as he would come as himself. I remember being dressed and coiffed by Douglas Trout and Petra von Katzen. I think I arrived as half-bride, half-groom inspired by the famous Erté design. All this in a small flat in Hurlingham where 150 people were crammed into four rooms. Freddie arrived with David Minns earlyish bearing a jeroboam of champagne: Moet and Chandon, of course! I think it was that night, in a haze, I first asked him to produce an album for me. I never thought that such an outrageous suggestion on my part would have been taken in let alone remembered through that veil of champagne bubbles.

Freddie didn't stay too long, probably about three quarters of an hour. He didn't like all those people crammed together although he enjoyed himself. We subsequently made arrangements to have lunch together and thereafter it seems we became mates. It's hard to remember and extricate definite dates and events as our lives from that point onwards became inextricably entangled. In other words, we hit it off.

It was Christmas 1975 when I was invited to see *Queen*'s now famous Hammersmith Christmas Concerts when *Bohemian Rhapsody* was at its zenith. Christmas Eve was the ultimate show. It might sound strange but I had never been to a real rock 'n' roll concert before. My life apart from theatre and theatrical musicals had been rooted in classical music and opera as my mother sang lieder. She took me to see Callas, Schwarzkopf, Fischer-Diskau and that's where my basics were developed. Watching Tony Bennett, Judy Garland and Dietrich had also given me my musical traditions of the more secular sort. Watching *Queen* and Freddie was a revelation especially as I had gotten to know Freddie as a friend but about whose professional life I knew little. Bearing in mind my own background, the theatre and sense of power generated by the guitar and the awesome audacity of the prancing peacock totally seduced me. It was wonderful stuff. Though some of the crassness repelled me, I was a willing convert to rock n' roll which, after all, is the very essence of this great band. Though I was doing concerts at the time, mine were so esoteric and eclectic that any comparison was invidious. Seeing Freddie and *Queen* opened up new vistas and possibilities for me within what I had already been doing which was so different to how Freddie performed.

In 1976, I and my band were appearing in Edinburgh for the first time on the official festival instead of my usual fringe activities doing a late night show at The Assembly Rooms in George Street. *Queen* as a band and their entourage came to see me as they had been performing at The Playhouse in David Evans' and John Reid's Festival of Popular Music. Those were the days when I was wearing designer gowns as well as raunchy street-wear to put over a show which encompassed everything from Jacques Brel, through Kurt Weill to Elton John as well as standards and new songs by Don Fraser and Malcolm Carrick. The real outrage of the show was my walking around the auditorium with a trolley dispensing champagne to the audience.

The show was a hit.

In retrospect, apart from liking my voice, Freddie realised at that point we were both performers, though he was very famous and I was relatively unknown. The difference didn't matter for I believe that as far as he was concerned, from that time on, although we could either criticise or compliment each other, we communicated.

As I've said, I used to live near the Hurlingham Tennis Club and was a keen tennis player. Clodagh Wallace, my manager, was a member of the Hurlingham Club and through her we had access to the courts. I used to play nearly every day in the summer and occasionally Freddie would join me. He'd certainly hit the ball jolly hard and was determined to get it not only over but in. However, he seemed to find it very difficult to move a lot and plainly expected the ball to come to him. Fortunately, there was always someone on hand to run after his balls!

The standard of his tennis wasn't up to that of his table tennis of which he was enormously proud and would talk about for ages. One day, however, our tennis careers hit a slight snag. We had often wondered why we were usually relegated to one of the back courts away from everyone. Surely it wasn't the standard of our game which was no worse than a lot of others.

Then, we finally discovered why and all was made clear in no uncertain terms. We received an edict from the club's governing body via my manager requesting that 'those two young men' should wear longer shorts.

Of course we used to go out a lot together too, everywhere from the opera, the ballet, as well as nightclubs and ordinary pubbing for however famous Freddie was he was no snob and enjoyed going where everyone else went. One particular night, after going to a few pubs – in a chauffeur driven car needless to say which made life so much easier – my band *Taxi* led by Michael Allison were performing at The Hog's Grunt at Production village in Cricklewood. Freddie and I decided to pay them a surprise visit. By the end of their set, after imbibing a little more, Freddie decided that we ought to do an impromptu version of *Jailhouse Rock*. Although it was one, and remained one, of Freddie's favourite songs, at the time I hardly knew more than the first line. Heavily prompted by the boys in the band and Freddie, we somehow managed to get through to a scrappy end.

Apparently a very private video exists of the ensuing performance and I have nightmares about the film emerging from obscurity at least once a week. By the end of the song, the audience still couldn't believe we were there and up on stage doing it and a couple of people had to come up to us to ask Freddie in sheer disbelief, "Are you really Freddie Mercury?" Still not convinced even after he had replied that he most certainly was, they probably still don't believe what happened in front of their very eyes to this day.

And off we sped into the night!

Much, much later when I was appearing at the Piccadilly Theatre in the West End with Carol Woods, Debby Bishop and Maria Friedman in *Blues in the Night*, Freddie, who had a continuous love affair with theatre would come on many occasions and just surprise us and turn up in the wings and watch the whole show. Afterwards, we would often go out for dinner and it happened that it was about this time he was doing the Montserrat Caballé *Barcelona* Album with Mike Moran and we were asked to appear on the album on the *Golden Boy* track.

It was at Christmas time and there was a singathon going on at the theatre which had been going on since midday and he again popped in just to see how it was all going. I was singing *River Deep Mountain High* which ostensibly he came to see. I was trying to persuade him that he too should appear on stage with me although he declined immediately, displaying his usual sincere reticence. After a drink or two and in the closing stages of the charity Singathon when the whole company was singing Christmas carols on stage, we sneaked on in the melée and together we did finally get to sing. Again, the audience were delightfully surprised.

What a wonderful Christmas we had!

NINA MYSKOW

Looking back, its funny that you can see a pattern or a shape to things. An essential strand of the continuous thread running through my life has been Elton, professionally, personally... I've met my best friends through Elton and, under these circumstances, Freddie.

I came down to London from Dundee having worked as the first female magazine editor in the DC Thomson organisation in 1978 and I started on Fleet Street as the rock writer on *The Sun*.

In February or March of the following year, 1979, I was invited to fly to Montreux in Switzerland to interview *Queen*. Just a few hours before I was due to go, I got a 'phone call from my uncle, telling me that my mother, who is very arthritic, had had a very bad fall and broken her thigh bone. She was to have major surgery the following day. I got into a complete panic, torn between cancelling the trip and doing my filial duty.

In the event, I went to Switzerland but in a terrible state and making it very clear to Paul Prenter who met the photographer and I at the airport that I was going to do the interview as fast as possible and then fly back directly to Scotland. This suddenly sounds a bit prima donna-ish but I was terribly upset about my mother. The extraordinary thing was that although the band had made a really special effort for me setting aside a whole day for the interview and photographs . Mary Austin and the other girls had organised and were cooking a special dinner after the interview. They seemed to understand my situation completely and were very sympathetic. I remember very little of the interview as I was mentally elsewhere. I always felt guilty about it. It was a job unfinished.

When *Queen* had a huge hit with *Flash Gordon* and I was asked to interview Freddie, I went with great trepidation to *Queen* Productions in Pembridge Road. I was shown into an upstairs room where Freddie was ensconced with, I think, a bottle of wine and two glasses. I thought to myself: "just go for it." I knew I had to make a special effort, remembering the 'handbag' incident and the Swiss disaster.

Within ten minutes, we were screaming with laughter. I don't know what it was but we just got on like a house on fire. We immediately clicked. I talked to him about his new house and he told me how much it cost. I asked if he had to have a mortgage for it and he paused, raised one eyebrow – the look again – and said, in ringing tones.

"Mortgage! *What*'s a mortgage, darling?"

We talked about whether he would ever settle down and he said:

"Absolutely not. When my legs give out, I'll be happy to just sit around in bandages, knitting socks for sailors!"

However, until that time came, it was obvious he was determined to enjoy himself.

After about an hour, perhaps less, a female minion put her head round the door and asked if there was anything we needed. This was obviously the rehearsed 'get-out' moment, the chance of escape if the interview was not going well. Freddie merely called for another bottle of wine. Even later, the poor girl appeared again, unable to believe the interview was still going on and asked twice if *everything* was alright.

"Oh, f... off, dear," said Freddie. "Just f... off!"

As the interview dragged drunkenly to a close, Freddie said commandingly:

"You've *got* to come to South America with us, darling. You've just *got* to come!" And so I went.

It was wonderful. The concerts there were just huge. Argentina had never seen anything like it in their lives. It was such an event in Buenos Aires that all airport announcements were suspended and when *Queen* arrived it was to the sound of their own albums blaring over the tannoys. Freddie loved it and gloated about all the people who must have been missing their planes through lack of information. Wherever the band went, they did so accompanied by huge, armoured, battleship-like personnel carriers bristling with machine guns poking through holes in the metal. Fleets of motorcycle cops sirened their way alongside the circus as it moved from one stadium to another.

The first gig in Buenos Aires was absolutely extraordinary. The Argentines are so passionate about football, they'd laid plastic sheeting over their entire precious pitch and there was a huge stage erected in the middle. There we were standing in front, ankle-deep in plastic.

By any standards it was a magnificent show. It just kind of exploded visually, with fireworks and musically, it was as about as perfect as you could get. Freddie's presence and charisma completely dominated the evening. At the end of the show, the Argentine flag was raised on one side of the stadium and the Union Jack on the other. It was very *Last Night Of The Proms*. I remember standing there in the darkness in the middle of this huge upsurge of emotion with tears pouring down my cheeks. I was just so bloody proud of them. Hard to believe that only a year later the two countries were at war.

I suppose there were about ten British journalists there. We were all staying at the Buenos Aires Sheraton and the following day, there was a reception thrown by the record company for all the press. Swans sculpted in ice on the buffet, the whole thing. I was totally startled. As soon as I walked into the room, Freddie grabbed my hand and said:

"Come and sit with me, dear. I don't want to talk to anyone else."

We plonked ourselves down at a table and started chattering and gossiping and laughing. I suppose it must have been very difficult for the other press to get a look in as they became totally excluded. One brave soul tried to nudge in, daring to sit down at the same table. Freddie refused to answer and would only reply through me. It was terribly embarrassing but then he was very wicked like that. He knew exactly what he was doing.

I must point out that by now I obviously had realised that the very daunting person I had first met in 1977 no longer put me off. I realised that 'the look' was merely a mask, a protective shell. However, I did love seeing him turning it on and giving someone else the full blast of that withering look of scorn.

I felt very drawn to him, not just because of the glamour, the talent and the outrage; the obvious things. It was his shyness and his vulnerability I found so attractive. It wasn't just the intelligence but also the warmth which you knew he didn't radiate to just anyone. Freddie would always remember what you'd said, as though it had really mattered to him and you kind of knew that only a few people knew that and it was a very precious secret that made you feel very privy to the heart of the man.

He left you thinking... Why me? Why am I sitting here next to him? It was a question that the other journalists must also have asked after that last night in Buenos Aires but for entirely different reasons.

After the concert, Freddie decided to take all of us out to dinner at what was supposed to be the best steak restaurant in town. We were flying off up to Rio the next day and it was the last chance for the hacks to get quotes from Freddie. It must have been very difficult for them. Without being rude to the other members of the band, all the editors wanted was Freddie and Freddie had refused to talk to any of the journalists, apart from me, that is.

We had the usual parade of police outriders and on the way to the restaurant we made a stop so that they could be photographed with Freddie. He loved it, of course, all those big blokes in all their leather gear. They were all grinning as though they were about to burst for Freddie was probably the biggest thing that had ever happened to them. I thought how nice of him to bother.

This restaurant was quite extraordinary. It was very close to Buenos Aires domestic airport and had a glass roof so planes took off practically over your dinner. It was terribly camp. I was very aware what a hard time the other journalists had had and felt rather guilty at hogging Freddie although I did so entirely at his request. As the party of twenty or so people entered the restaurant, I kind of held back so that they could make a mad rush to sit as close to him as they could. He was sitting right in the middle of a long table, with his back against the wall. He was looking up and, I realised, looking for me. When he found me and caught my eye, he waved his right hand imperiously and pointed at the seat directly opposite. I raised my eyebrows and gestured feebly at the ravening pack of hacks around me. Freddie rolled his eyes upwards, sighed and mouthed: "F... 'em, darling!" and pointed again at the seat. What could I do? I shrugged, rather embarrassed, at the others and sat down, very happily, I admit. It was a triumphant moment and should have been accompanied by *The Ride of the Valkyries*.

It was such an amazing night that when we returned to the

Sheraton at three o'clock on a Monday morning, we didn't feel like going to bed at all. Dennis Davidson, the PR, was catching the 8 a.m. flight to Rio de Janeiro to set things up for our arrival later that night so we told him it was ludicrous to go to bed at all. He didn't. I wish Freddie had been involved but he was elsewhere by this time. We sat in the coffee shop drinking Bloody Marys, waved Dennis off and were still there drinking Bloody Marys not only at breakfast but also as people arrived for lunch. Little did we realise how disastrous that was. Unbeknownst to me, Phil Symes had organised an interview with Brian May at 3 p.m. I did it, although I don't know how and it *was* a damn good interview. I had to contend with the fact that Brian was predisposed against me, a fact he brought up after twenty minutes. He'd hated the 'Flash' Freddie feature I'd done earlier but by the end of our interview, he'd softened and confessed that he quite liked me and that I was completely different from what he'd imagined. Amazing, but I don't think he ever guessed that I was completely drunk. It's remarkable how you can sober up when you have to.

The press pack went rocketing off up to Rio and, fortified by even more alcohol on the plane, went off with Dennis Davidson to our hotel's Carnival Fiesta Ball, which is where my American Express Card exploded once and forever... Dennis had ordered a couple of bottles of champagne. We were soon completely immersed in the daft atmosphere; everyone round us was samba-ing in two spangles and a wisp and completely rat-arsed. I ordered two more bottles of champagne and paid for them on my American Express Card. I was obviously at the stage where my signature dribbled off onto the tablecloth. I could have been doodling for all I cared, added to which, we'd just come from Argentina which had thousands of noughts in the currency and here we were in Brazil where there were even more zeros. I checked nothing. When the bill came in three months later, I discovered that for the two bottles of champagne, I'd been charged three hundred and seventy pounds. That's the effect of Freddie for you! I've never had an American Express Card since. Though I blame him entirely, I do feel rather proud. If you're going to go out, go out with a bang!

Live Aid was another event where I was incredibly proud of him and what he did for British rock 'n' roll. He sort of took charge of the world that afternoon. I was particularly thrilled because all those repellent music papers had for years been rather disdainful towards *Queen*, dubbing their music 'pomp rock' in a very disparaging way. There was a feeling going round that *Queen* were all flash and no substance.

When Freddie came on stage, I can remember standing there in the stadium absolutely transfixed. It's an extraordinary feeling being part of a crowd of thousands of people all feeling the same thing, experiencing the same emotion. At *Live Aid*, the feeling was even more heightened as you were obviously joining with millions more around the world. I think it was that performance whereby Freddie finally established himself, once and for all, as the consummate live performer. He seemed to embody the very meaning of the word 'charisma'. God, I loved him for it and I was so proud. He was almost like a matador, challenging, defying anyone not to succumb, not to be swept along by him. What a star, for that day he really was the champion of the world.

After Wembley, the *Live Aid* broadcast continued from several points including Legends nightclub in Mayfair. I remember having a long conversation with Brian but I don't remember seeing Freddie there.

Although the South American tour had given me a firmer relationship with *Queen*, I was startled as well as delighted to get an invitation to Freddie's fortieth birthday party at his house in Logan Place on Sunday, September 7th 1986. It was to be a Mad Hatters' theme party. I remember panicking slightly about this, 'cos I'm not a hat person. I'm too short and the sort of hats that suit my face make me look like a mushroom. I took with me a journalist friend called Les Daly, whom I'd known since my DC Thomson days in Dundee. He's now the assistant editor of the *Sunday Times* colour supplement. It was a magic day. The sun was shining and once beyond the green door in the wall, we were in a different world. Everything had been organised down to the last detail. I can remember the flunkies with white-painted faces coming round with little chequerboard sandwiches, served from vast top hats. It was all very Alice-in-Wonderland. We all drank an incredible amount and I fear I did one of my party tricks. I taught Jim Beach's children how to make water bombs which I'd learned from the Rupert Annual when I was four. I met Jim a couple of years ago and he was still cursing me for it. Patti Mostyn, Elton's Australian PR-cum-bridesmaid was so drunk, it was only the fact that her heels were embedded in the lawn which kept her upright. It was lovely for me to see the house that Freddie had described all those years before, complete with minstrels' gallery.

He took Les and me and Anita Dobson on the Grand Tour, finishing up on the balcony outside his bedroom where we stood drinking champagne and taking in the party in the garden beneath. He was very happy and proud and he had every reason to be. Brian was wearing a sombrero the size of a flying saucer and extremely tight black velvet flares which his wife kept telling me were ten years old. I believed her. If that was the day that Brian met Anita, I'm firmly convinced those trousers must have had a lot to do with it.

As we stood on that balcony, Freddie pointed to the house across the street and proudly told me that Diana Rigg lived there. You'd imagine a star as big as Freddie wouldn't be impressed by his neighbours but he was. Stars need their stars too.

MIKE MORAN

After *Time*, Freddie very directly asked me to be involved in co-producing a record with him. He'd always wanted to do a cover version and decided upon *The Great Pretender* which we started in the studios I have at home and finished off at The Townhouse.

He was in something of a quandary as to how to end the song... I had a few ideas but as I tested each one he merely pronounced limply:

"Very good, dear."

I just knew it was not up to scratch. The ending just got longer and longer and seemed never to reach an end. He urged me to "do a few flashy bits, dear." He loved anything technically virtuoso. It was then he came up with Paganini... That was the key to the problem. From that as a starting point, I went into a violin arrangement that eventually ended the record.

The mix saw our roles being somewhat reversed. Dave Richards, *Queen*'s producer, came into London to mix the track at the Townhouse. I was rather nervous and very concerned about what was after all my co-production. The mix went on and so did my neurotic attention to every tiny teeny detail. On and on and on until Fred could stand it no longer.

"For God's sake, leave it alone. Let's f... off home, dear. You're doing a me!"

He was thrilled when the record went straight into the top five.

"That's what I like, dear. Straight in, up to the top and then out!"

He was thrilled. For those of you who know the video for *Pretender*, I shall say no more... Only Freddie could have made that entrance.

It seemed to be the season for re-releases and covers. He was rather concerned that he would be labelled as just following the crowd. There was ultimately no danger of that, of course; no danger of comparison whatsoever.

As a performer, he was totally instinctive and original. Being on stage with this somewhat diminutive figure was amazing. He made you think he was a tall, big man. Before a performance, he was often a mess. People couldn't go near him. He consciously psyched himself up, spending ages in front of the mirror, making himself up as part of the psych process. When Freddie was ready to go on-stage, there had been an incredible transformation. On-stage, the power he generated and radiated was immense. If he should, God forbid, pick up on a mistake on-stage, he would flash you 'that look' and it would be withering. Really intimidating.

Rehearsing *Barcelona* on-stage with Montserrat Caballé, Freddie forgot she too was a seasoned performer. He was ultimately shocked to the core that her tiny presence, so understated in rehearsal, encroached on his larger, wider more expansive performance. At the beginning of the rehearsal he whispered aside to me: "I'll tone it down, dear," assuming he was going to overpower her. Little did he know that she, of course, like all divas, was saving herself for the real thing not just a rehearsal. At the performance, she rose to the occasion, soaring into form and assuming the colossal presence of a legend. Mr. Mercury was shocked. He realised that he had no need whatsoever to 'tone it down'...

That Ibiza performance of *Barcelona* was well-publicised but no one expected the triumph it became. It was the acid-house summer of '87 and everyone had come expecting to see this rock concert at the Ku nightclub. *Duran Duran, Spandau Ballet.* No one could quite understand this thing with Montserrat and Freddie. What they eventually got, this meeting of two legends, they just weren't bargaining for. There were people crying, tears rolling down the faces of this Latin crowd where raw emotion is everything. It was an act no one could hope to emulate.

"Let 'em try and follow that!" said Freddie as he came offstage.

Actually I've jumped a bit, haven't I? This Montserrat and Freddie part of my life had begun one day about three in the morning. I was in my car when Freddie contacted me to tell me that Montserrat Caballé wanted to meet him. He insisted on my going with him and we arranged a date to fly off to Barcelona to meet her. The meeting had happened because he'd been in Spain previously and had announced on Spanish media that he was a big fan of hers. Either she or someone in her family heard the interview and hey presto. Wheels were set in motion. Now we were landing in Barcelona and driving to the Ritz to actually meet her.

Freddie was in a lather of nerves. He wanted to take something to play to her, something she would not have already heard via her children. We booked a private dining room in the Ritz. In comes, almost like the Queen of Sheba, Montserrat and entourage. Bit awkward at first as no one knew each other but Freddie plunged straight in; such a courageous man. He told her he would make her laugh and played her the track that he and I had written which was his impression of her singing, the track that was the B side of *The Great Pretender.* She was amazed...

"You seeng like mezzo soprano, no?"

"Thank you, dear," said Freddie.

"Eet eez you?"

"It is me," Freddie admitted.

"Wonderful," she enthused, "I shall give it a world premiere in three weeks time at Covent Garden... "

There was a moment's silence before she tapped me on the shoulder and announced:

"And *you* shall play!"

She then demanded that Freddie write her a song, a special song just for herself to sing in Barcelona for her Catalan homeland.

The waiters and staff at the Ritz couldn't believe this meeting between two such superstars. After our meeting, I wanted to write out something for Montserrat before we left the Ritz. The Maître d' said we could use the piano in the restaurant. By this time it was getting on for eight o'clock in the evening. I suddenly was aware of people milling round with cutlery and tablecloth. I checked with the Maître d' what was happening and if I was in the way. He asked me if I was indeed the gentleman who was writing some music for La Caballé. I replied I was. "Then the others can wait!" he replied.

When Montserrat left the Ritz that night, Freddie turned round and said:

"What *have* we done, dear?"

"We?" I said...

"What about *me*? I've got to play for her at Covent Garden, for God's sake."

In London, I wrote out a part for her before the concert at the Opera House. The night before, we saw her in one of the Covent Garden rehearsal rooms. Freddie was very, very nervous. Montserrat rattled off the song, reading it with blithe professionalism, the strangeness of the material being no obstacle. Wondering where to include the song in her set, Freddie suggested she do it for her encore.

"Which one?" she demanded grandly, "I usually do at leeest six!"

Freddie's jaw visibly dropped.

On the night, Freddie was panicking in my dressing room. He was making me so nervous that I ordered him out of the room. Where he went, I don't know but she led me out on-stage as she took her bow. Even from the stage, I could see Freddie, frozen to the spot as Montserrat explained that her next song was one which I and Freddie Mercury had written for her. Then she sang and it went like a dream. Everyone stood and applauded.

Afterwards, Freddie was fussing round her like an old hen and couldn't believe that I'd been able to just walk on and perform a song cold, for the first time. When we got back to Freddie's house, Carlos, Montserrat's brother, announced the diva couldn't stay that long... At five o'clock in the morning we just had to kick her out. She had hardly been able to wait to get dinner over and get to the piano with Freddie. We played everything from Aretha Franklin to Jennifer Holliday and Montserrat had a go at gospel music like a diva had never done before. She felt a wonderful sense of artistic freedom which Freddie brought into her life. She said that it was wonderful being with people for whom music was a very natural expression rather than a ritualised process.

As soon as we got back to London from Barcelona, the solo project he had wanted me to help him on was therefore shelved from then on as he first embarked on the composition of the song she had demanded which turned into *Barcelona* and then into generating other songs which turned into working on a whole album.

"She wants something about Barcelona," I said, "what's a good starting point?"

"Well, dear," he said, "I suppose we should just sing something..." and he merely opened his mouth and sang "Barcelona..."

"Oh," I said, "that's rather good." The start of it was as simple as that.

By the end of a day we'd got the main bones of the song. Typically Freddie, everything was then explored and expanded and extended into what stands now as a monumental production.

Freddie hadn't been able to believe that he was going to sing with Montserrat Caballé. I remember him being very excited on the plane back from Barcelona after we'd first met her. We began to talk seriously about what was ahead. I had done a lot of work already with well-known opera singers and tried to explain to Freddie something of the restrictions he was about to encounter, restrictions of the way formally trained singers interpret and express. I warned Freddie he would never in a million years get Montserrat to sing in any style approaching rock 'n' roll. He realised very soon that we had a very difficult brief, writing songs which showed off the best of both performers yet without compromising either of their opposite styles and techniques. Writing and recording *Barcelona* was one thing. To write a whole album proved hugely demanding. There would certainly *never* have been a follow-up.

"Never again, dear!" he pronounced with relief when the album was finally put to bed.

Even after the songs were written, the vocals were put on entirely separately. Freddie would put down Montserrat's part for our convenience singing falsetto, just to see where and how the songs were progressing.

Fallen Priest was a song which I started while Freddie was recording the video for *Pretender*. I played it to him after one of the *Pretender* shoots and he was ecstatic about it. He realised that the Montserrat project was indeed feasible from that time on and thrilled that he could now see an overview of the album's direction. After *Priest*, he played another idea, a little piece of Japonisme beneath which I put some harmonies and which turned into La Japonaise. Kaz Watanabe helped out with the Japanese part of the recording and Freddie was always being corrected.

"Who cares!" he stormed one day, "so you stress it wrongly and you're f...ing the cat instead of conquering the world! Who cares!"

In the studio, I constantly experiment; I never used to tape things. As a result, good ideas can, like sand, often slip through the fingers as I would often temporarily forget what I'd just played. Fred would be furious:

"You're always doing that to me! You play all these wonderful things and you can never f...ing remember them!"

He, on the other hand, did have a wonderful memory. He could remember every note. He even carried a little book in which he wrote everything down that was really important to him, even sketching things. He was insistent that certain things be recorded. "Write it in the book, dear!"

On the Montserrat album, I recall a wonderful example of Freddie's superb knowledge and instinct for harmony and melody. He was after something different, as usual, and suddenly turned round and asked me to turn a multi-track tape over and play it backwards. He didn't want to repeat the section already recorded but needed a development. I did as he asked and he then went out into the studio and immediately put down a vocal completely ad lib over the reversed tape and this in fact is the surviving melody on the track, *The Fallen Priest*.

One of the big difficulties in making the Monserrat album was pinning her down as far as schedule was concerned. Opera singers are notoriously booked up, years in advance. She would jet in from somewhere on her way to somewhere else and we'd maybe have a couple of hours. Everyone was screaming for the album to be finished and we had to seriously get her to commit to definite sessions, rather than slotting in between her big gigs. Montsie, Montserrat's niece who acted as her P.A. was consulted as to what Madame was doing the week we wanted her.

"You are in Russia," Montsie announced on consulting her diary.

"Cancel Russia," ultimated the diva and we got our sessions.

Freddie and Montserrat formed a very real bond. Freddie and I were invited to attend a tribute evening to Montserrat at the Madrid Opera House. I was asked to play *Ensueno* for her. It was like an operatic *This is Your Life*, all unrehearsed. Huge luminaries were due to attend – di Stefano, Carreras, Juan Pons. I was announced and duly went on-stage with Montserrat and she sang *Ensueño*.

"Eez Freddie here?" she hissed at me in a stage whisper as we took our bow.

"Yes," I replied and pointed him out.

At the end of the show, she insisted he be on stage with her. It was a tremendous vindication for him. Like Montserrat, Freddie was deeply respectful of talented people, those whom he admired in whatever field. He was always ready to accord credit where he felt credit was due and when it was done in reverse, when he was the recipient, he was delighted.

JACKY GUNN

We send out four issues of the fan club magazine annually. The band were supposed to take it in turns. I remembered Freddie hadn't done one for ages. As he'd told us to call him if there were any problems, I rang the house. Peter Freestone, Freddie's P.A., answered and sounded very unsure as to whether Freddie would acquiesce. However, much to Peter's surprise, Freddie agreed to do it. We then arranged for Freddie to do the Christmas issue every year. I graduated to being able to talk to him on the 'phone. He never seemed to think that anything he'd done or was doing was interesting enough and always asked for advice as to what he should say. But he always left writing it to the last moment. One week would go by, then another and the deadline approached. Then he would realise he *had* to do it and he'd get down to it.

"Well, I'll just have to stay up late, dear, won't I!"

At parties we would talk about the fan situation. He was always interested, especially how many fan club members there were. Numbers talk, he loved. He helped a lot. As much as he could. He was always there when you needed him, even for silly things like 'What does Freddie have for breakfast?'

From thinking I was going to be working for a band led by an ogre, I was very pleased to be able to get to know a really great guy. People were incredulous when I said that the Freddie I knew was a very warm, kind and caring man. Fans often seemed not to want to know this. They almost didn't want him to be human. Lots said they didn't ever want to meet him, preferring to keep him on a pedestal.

When I knew I'd clicked, that I was really a part of the team, it was one Christmas; 1985, I think. We'd been to Shezan for the office party.

"Back to my place, dear," Freddie announced and we all piled back to the kitchen at Logan Place drinking champagne and having a great time until six o'clock in the morning. There were a whole lot of us. The next thing we knew, the cleaning ladies were ringing the bell at nine thirty. We were putting the world to rights, solving all the world's problems. Politics, who should be in power, what we'd each do if we had the power. Usual stuff when you had the confidence of a great chat. Suddenly he turned to me and said:

"I shouldn't be talking like this in front of you, dear. You work for me!"

I giggled and asked to use the 'phone.

"Why?" he demanded.

"Because I work for you and I'm supposed to be at the office."

"Tell them you're with me," he commanded.

Every year, the Fan Club convenes at Pontins. We've had seven of these conventions so far. Fifteen hundred fans turn up and we show *Queen* videos, play tapes and records. Its a great fun weekend, the first of which, in April 1986, was at Great Yarmouth on a caravan site. Chris

Taylor was going to come, Roger's P.A. and we were going to have a charity auction of *Queen* things. A T-shirt from Freddie, something else from the others.

Just before we left London for Great Yarmouth, there was a call for me at the office. Freddie was on the line: "This... *thing*, dear..."

"Do you mean the convention?" I ventured.

"Yes. Have you got enough, dear? Enough stuff?"

"Well, we could always do with more," I said.

"Then how about a leotard. Hyde Park, dear. Made for me. Diamond-studded crutch. Only one. Would you like it?"

Would I *like* it?

"When are you going, dear?"

"Tomorrow," I replied.

"Well, darling... Whatever you do, do it with style."

I was on cloud nine. It was wonderful vindication of a lot of hard work.

JIM JENKINS

A whole gang of us went over to Paris in 1979 for the three French shows. No gigs were planned for England on that tour. When we got to the gig, we asked Chris Taylor if he'd ask Freddie to ring a bicycle bell for us during the show. We'd taken a load of silly bicycle bells to ring when they played *Bicycle Race.* Crystal came back and we asked what reaction he'd got.

"He didn't say a thing," Crystal said. We'd given him a bell to hand over and we all noticed it hadn't come back. So, on with the show.

When it came time for *Bicycle Race,* the show stopped. The music actually just stopped. Freddie got up from the piano and came over to where we were standing carrying our bicycle bell. He bent down and rang it loudly and said: "You're mad!" and went back to the piano and carried on with the show as if nothing had happened. Our gang of fans from that moment on became known as The Royal Family; he called us "My Royal Family" once.

At those shows we were always in the front row. We made a point of it. The French were most put out as we raced over the chairs to get those seats. Every night we were there to the extent where Freddie would look down at the front rows and shake his head in complete disbelief. But he was thrilled. He told Vicky and Amanda to thank us all specially for coming over.

In 1982, a friend and I went over to California for the shows on that tour. The Americans didn't seem to like the funky image the band were doing then. Basically it was the *Hot Space* album. The band therefore decided to drop those kind of tracks and did the harder ones...*Put Out The Fire,* things like that. That went down very well. The Americans of course thought of *Queen* as a heavy rock band. That's what they wanted and that's what they were expecting. When they didn't get it, the reaction of the audience was not good. For example, there was no feedback from the audience when Freddie started his sing-along-with-Fred time. It was Brian's guitar that really got them going. That was San Francisco.

It was the same in Los Angeles. The band were supposed to do four shows and yet only did two. The last show in L.A. was superb and sadly it was the last time the band played in North America. I was really upset when I returned to England. I had been expecting to see great shows. A friend had written and said how wonderful *Queen* concerts were over there. It was just that there had been no real audience reaction. I should have gone a couple of years earlier.

In Hollywood, I met Freddie in the hotel he was staying in, The Beverly Wilshire. We had a photo taken together. The following year, the *Radio GaGa* video was made with all the fans. I took the L.A. photo with me to be autographed. He took it, looked at it and then patted my stomach and said, "You're putting on too much weight, dear."

A few months later, they did the *I Want to Break Free* video. I always found Freddie very relaxed at the shoots and I always found him very approachable. I got a call that Freddie wanted six guys to dress up as miners so we came down to London, to Limehouse, to the video shoot. Freddie was in a great mood and he was in wonderful humour. There we were standing in the cave, dressed as miners in helmets. He took off his red dressing gown and stepped back into the midst of us. He banged into my helmet and he jumped forward.

"It's okay, Freddie. Its only my helmet."

"Shut up, dear," he replied.

We then started chatting about his throat nodules which were troubling him at the time. It was also when he had shaved off his moustache and I had the temerity to say:

"Oh, we've got our old Freddie back," and added, "now you've shaved off your moustache you might write some decent songs again."

He glared. I went cold. If looks could kill, I wouldn't be here today. He hated that remark and marched off saying:

"Are *all* you people in Liverpool still mad?"

I said, "Yeah!" I never meant that what I said should be hurtful. It just came out. The friends I was with told me I shouldn't have said what I'd said. Still, he can't have been that upset as he allowed us to remain in the studio to see the filming of the ballet bit.

PAUL GAMBACCINI

Since Freddie's death I've had occasions when I've thought about all the one-on-one times I'd spent with him. At all those times he was just that, utterly one-on-one. He always had this air of authority and professionalism, charisma; but he was always very direct, with me.

When somebody trusts you, you can understand their shyness as far as the eyes of the world are concerned. He said to me that one day we'd do an interview that would reveal all and shock the world. I've always thought that the reason he never did interviews in the seventies was that he didn't want to be quizzed about his sex life. I feel he didn't want to come out completely. It was only when people like Boy George did, around that time, which gave him the confidence.

In America, I'm convinced the decline in *Queen*'s fortunes came at the time the *Body Language* album came out. I think it was the only bad career move *Queen* made and it was one from which they never recovered in the USA, although *Radio GaGa* was a top twenty hit. There has been speculation that Freddie's clone look was the cause of the band's demise in the USA. It can't be. The clone look, the 'out' Freddie look, was already on *The Game* album which was their biggest seller and which generated two number one singles. The gay backlash theory just doesn't hold water. It was just that their U.S. audience didn't like the disco thing that the *Body Language* album contained.

He played me his solo album so excitedly. He still wanted to succeed as a solo artist. He asked me what tracks in my opinion should be singles. I was struck that even though *Queen* were so massively successful as a group, Freddie was still hungry for a further and different kind of success. I'm convinced that no matter how long he lived, he would always have wanted new challenges and new successes.

I really would like to say how kind he was too. There was once a party and my boyfriend came with me; I wanted to leave early and I went looking for my boyfriend with whom I'd come and there he was, in the bedroom, on the bed with another guy. Freddie saw me and saw how horrified I was. He helped me immediately and with him, I was able to march into the bedroom to rout the other man. Freddie was always very solicitous about my relationship. He cared very deeply about our personal lives, was very concerned that we should be as happy as possible. We spoke as forthrightly as people with nothing to hide can. We would often meet in one of two clubs, Legends or Heaven, the discotheque owned by Richard Branson. Legends was more social, obviously. Freddie would usually be with Straker. Campbell Palmer, such a generous host at Legends, would ply us with drinks and one day said to Straker:

"Oh, Peter! You're so talented; *You* should be a star too!"

Cringe! The comparison was utterly embarrassing with Freddie standing next to him.

Freddie's shyness often dictated behaviour which was interpreted as imperial. He would often appear to hide away, selecting those whom he wished to join him.

The high life he lived really passed me by. There was only one occasion at his home where I saw drugs being available. It was not obvious that he did use drugs and he never let it show publicly in his behaviour unlike many others. He presented to the public at all times an image divorced of all personal connections. If you hadn't been with him, you'd never have known.

1984 I remember talking to him in Heaven and I asked Freddie if he'd changed his behaviour at all in view of the growing health crisis. Of course, in those days we didn't even know what it was we weren't supposed to do to stay healthy. He used to tell me about all the clubs and places he went to in New York. With a sweep of his arm he told me:

"My attitude is F... it, darling, I'm doing everything with every-one."

From that moment on Freddie was, sadly, high on my risk list. As a New Yorker, I knew only too well what that meant. The drug use and the lifestyle affected the body which can only take so much.

He loved being in the position to host people and he also loved being the head of the table. Not for nothing did he have such a large dining table. I enjoyed his love of culture too. I remember seeing him at a Montserrat Caballé recital before he ever become involved with her and he was really excited.

In the nickname tradition, I was once almost dubbed by Freddie. I've always been called Gambo so there was no need for me to be embroiled in the 'naming' game. Freddie announced one night that I was henceforth to be called Gina.

"Why?" I demanded.

"After Gina Lollobrigida," he said.

Thank God no one except Straker ever picked up on that and I never had to suffer public christening. On the other hand, I have to say that his dubbing of Michael Jackson as 'Mahalia' was brilliant.

I have always used *Queen* in my discussions with young groups as the model of how to conduct a career. I cannot imagine four more different individuals. They were determined to stay together because they realised that their chemistry was unique and worth preserving. My hat has always been off to all of them for being that tolerant and understanding of each other.

GORDON ATKINSON

I remember lots of things.

I remember going to Freddie's flat in Stafford Terrace one very hot summer's afternoon and having tea in the patio garden. He'd told me on the 'phone before I arrived that his roses were covered with greenfly and I came bearing an aerosol spray which he took, and danced up and down in front of every rose spraying avidly. However, when death and destruction had been disbursed, he became stricken with remorse about the number of insects that must have died. It was as though in fact he would, after all, have preferred his roses covered with live insects rather than littered with dead ones.

The weekend my friend and I spent in Montreux, we were directed by Freddie to walk by the lake and examine the gardens. He 'produced' the entire weekend. What to wear, where to walk, what to see... Everything down to the last detail even to the tie one would be wearing in the restaurant that Saturday evening, a meal which was to be the highlight of the weekend. He actually got me to show him the suit I'd brought with me. As instructed, we walked along the lakeside looking at the gardens between the mahonia trees which were in full bloom. There were some large brown eagles swooping and soaring over the lake. It was wonderful with the ferries plying back and forth. Almost timeless.

We went on the Saturday night to the restaurant Freddie Giradet after a great deal of telephoning and haggling for it is notoriously difficult to get into. There were to be about twenty courses, everything deliciously and perfectly small. It was Swiss adaptation of French cuisine. There were twelve of us around the table that night including Barbara Valentino. Claud Nobs was also there, the concert promoter who chose local Swiss wine at Freddie's request to accompany each course. It was a meal orchestrated to perfection.

We had been to Claud Nobs' villa the night before after a meal at the Station Hotel; Claud showed us wonderful videos projected on a huge screen. He had a vast video and film library in the basement of his house. I remember Freddie specially requested an Aretha Franklin video which was duly sought and shown.

On the way to Claud's villa, Freddie suggested I ride with Jim Beach and I have to say I have never been so frightened in my life. Of course, Freddie had known how I would feel all along... He knew perfectly well how Jim Beach drove! We screeched round corners on two wheels, it was like a movie, as though Jim was *trying* to make me sick. I expected it to be an enterprising drive but it was like some crazed dodgem ride. Whatever it was that Freddie was working on in the studio at that time, we never knew. He always kept his working life very separate from his social activities.

I remember a night at Covent Garden where Wayne Eagling had choreographed . There was a fault in the tape of the musique concréte and the company had to start again. The set was composed of little pyramids, like *Last Year at Marienbad.* After ten minutes, the ballet recommenced. Freddie was terribly distraught. I think Lady Di was there as well; someone like that. It was a similar evening to when we had all gone to see Placido Domingo sing *Otello.* Anyway, it was the failure of the technical production which Freddie felt so very deeply and acutely, almost as if something had gone wrong with one of his own shows. He couldn't bear to think of his close friend being compromised by technical and mechanical failure. In a situation like that he always kept his head. He felt Wayne's predicament very sensitively.

He approached his illness in his own perfectionistic way, discussing pros and cons of the various forms of treatment quite objectively with the various specialists from the Westminster Hospital. He never allowed his physical condition to interfere with his professional commitments. At the time he made the video of *Barcelona* with Montserrat Caballé, his haemoglobin had fallen to 7.0 grammes (fifty percent of a normal reading) and yet he went ahead and shot *Barcelona* like the true professional he was.

At the party Freddie gave at Pikes hotel on Ibiza for his forty first birthday celebration in 1987, our plane was the first to leave Heathrow after an air traffic controllers' strike. Freddie had chartered the plane for his friends and there were many famous names on board including Anita Dobson, Wayne Sleep, Wayne Eagling and Francesca Thyssen. It was champagne all the way after the initial demonstration of how to save ourselves in the event of a disaster. The only disaster would have been if the plane had run out of champagne.

Arriving at Pikes, I was allocated the bridal suite in which the decor was entirely black and where we were exhorted not to use the air conditioning system as to do so would have caused a major power failure. We quickly changed into our swimming trunks and went up to sit by the pool. It was the nicest part of the weekend for me. We stayed for two hours in the dying evening sunlight before the festivities began. Freddie was at his most relaxed but still looking forward to the evening ahead with characteristic enthusiasm. There were to be three hundred guests although a thousand eventually turned up. The highlight of the evening was a firework spectacular, culminating in a set piece which spelled out "Happy Birthday Freddie" in flames which he adored.

"Well, follow *that* one, dear!" he yelled out as he watched the sparkling spectacle.

Throughout the party, he circulated amongst his guests enquiring most solicitously and individually if people were having a good time, whether they'd had enough to eat and drink. He was a wonderful host, always.

DAVID MUNNS

After gigs, when he was touring, he'd show up to dinners afterwards. He was always up about things; never depressed. The only time I ever saw him kind of depressed was when the real punk thing was at its height. He was on tour in the U.K., Glasgow or somewhere like that. He told me he didn't really understand the punk thing. We had a long chat about that. It was all horrible to him; it wasn't music to him. I just said he had to look at the good things in it 'cos there are good things. Its only the kids telling you what they want. I told him it would settle down to its place in the market. It was a difficult time for him.

The next *Queen* sleeve that came out was a lot of leather, jeans and singlets, leather hats and things. Freddie always picked up on things going on around him and he adapted it to what he knew he could convey. He knew he had to change and adapt, much more than many writers and performers to make sure that he could fit himself in with the changed scene.

I moved to Capitol in Canada at the time when the band started with the horrible records. *Body Language*, that record killed *Queen* in America. Then in 1983, *Queen* left Warners and moved back to Capitol and suddenly there was Roger in Toronto promoting and talking about his own solo record and *The Works* which became a platinum album in Canada. I never really thought that the American public ever understood *Queen*. They saw *Queen* as essentially a rock band with an unusual lead singer rather than as the unique band they were who had something different to offer.

I returned to England in 1984 to EMI. Freddie was free from CBS as far as his solo work was concerned. I resumed my relationship with *Queen*. Freddie wanted to do *The Great Pretender*, we went along with it and it was a huge hit. *It's a Kind of Magic* was going to be the sound track for *The Highlander*. Bob Mercer was at EMI Films and he showed the film to Freddie and Jim Beach. Roger wrote *It's a Kind of Magic* which got stuck at number two for ages. They so wanted it to be number one but sadly it never got there. The band had, however, got it all back again. The live record of *Live Magic* recorded on that summer's tour came out and it sold over half a million albums in a month. Huge.

Then I left EMI and went to Polydor. It was round about then that EMI weren't for some reason very interested in Freddie's ambitions for a solo career.

Then Freddie had the idea for the record with Montserrat Caballé and Jim Beach came to me. I was always into Freddie's apparently crazy ideas, always had been. *Barcelona* was a huge hit, though the album didn't sell all that well, its a pity he's not around now to see what is going to happen to it this coming summer, over the time of the Olympics. I saw Freddie a few times over that album but basically I never saw him much again.

I went to that birthday party in Ibiza. Freddie threw the best parties in the record business. Him and *Queen*.

It's very hard to keep a band together in the record business like they did. For me, they were always a band. They were a real rock 'n' roll band. See the way they work on stage, Roger drumming and singing, Deacon keeping everyone's metre going... they were wonderful as a unit. Lot of those songs became better records because nothing was ever suppressed. They were all equally important. They must have had the right kind of personalities to stick with it.

No one ever left.

PETER HINCE

Queen were looking for a new crew and they'd asked *Mott's* roadies, Mott having split up and so had the re-formed *Mott*, to come and work for them. Ritchie and Phil were brought in, probably by John Harris the sound engineer/crew boss, and then I was brought in to look after John and Freddie. It was summer 1975 when they were still recording *A Night At The Opera* and around the time of the change-over of management. I had previously been asked to be Brian's roadie at the time of their first trip to Japan as his then roadie had threatened to quit but as he later decided to stay, the meeting I'd had with the tour manager at Trident was all in vain.

I wanted to work for *Queen* because in those days they were touring a lot and they were going to places I'd never been. When we first decided to go and work for *Queen* we had to go and blag all three albums and we had to listen to them to get familiar with it all.

The first tour I did with *Queen* was the U.K. *Bo Rhap* tour which was at the end of 1975. Both the single and the album were number one. Band and crew always travelled separately. On that tour we all got busted leaving Newcastle to travel to Dundee. Both crew and band buses. Someone had tipped off the police, probably a gopher who'd been sacked off the tour. The police obviously thought it was going to be some huge heroin cache. There was a massive police operation but only three people were apprehended, two for minimal amounts of amphetamines and one for a possession of a roach end. I had to roll up my sleeve to be searched for needle marks. Freddie was brought in wearing his short fur coat. There he was with his make-up bag and his black nails.

"Do you take drugs, Mr. Mercury?"

"Don't be so impertinent, you stupid little man!" barked Fred.

Drugs were very, very taboo in those days amongst the band. That tour was really, really hard work. Some days, we were doing two shows a night, seven and nine. They were adding extra shows all the way as it was so sold out. They couldn't add extra dates so it was extra shows. We were all exhausted. But we were all a lot younger then.

On those early tours, the only times I'd ever really see Fred was at sound checks and the shows. The band were all very diligent, they all turned up well on time, sometimes even earlier than they were called. They were very disciplined and hard-working then. Particularly Freddie. He never considered money. If something wasn't working, he would immediately order another new one. Everything had to be the best, to do the best work.

If something was wrong, the monitors or anything to do with faulty pyrotechnics, I'd get the full brunt of his wrath in those days even though the failures were nothing to do with me. I understood his frustrations, even though he would scream and shout in terrible rage on stage. The monitors were usually the cause of his rages and someone was ultimately found to take complete charge of the monitor system for it was terribly important. Later, as we were so trusted, we were assigned certain tasks to make sure that every cue worked precisely to achieve the production effects.

Their dedication was intense for indeed, quite unashamedly, they wanted to be the biggest band in the world. Everything and anything was sacrificed for perfectionism and quality. Quality came before anything.

As the years went by, the tautness of the discipline both of the band and it's members slackened off but whenever crisis loomed, whenever it seemed that things were falling apart either on stage or in the studio, it was always Freddie who would hold things together, pull things together. Anywhere and any time a Captain was required, it was always Freddie who fulfilled that role. He dragged it out of the others; when they hadn't played together for six months or whatever and a performance was required, Freddie would get it out of them. He was aware of everything, lighting, the set. He carried so much in his head and knew when a thing wasn't going right.

He hated being alone. He had to have someone with him either physically or at least in the next room if we were staying in hotels. He never travelled alone either. We were recording in Munich once and both Freddie and I had had to come back to London for whatever reasons. On Freddie's return journey there was none to accompany him; except me. So along came the first class tickets and off I went to the airport only to find there was some kind of strike on. I hung around seemingly forever whilst Freddie stayed at home until the last call for the flight was made and only then did he appear. I met him at the door, checked him in and we were whisked through to board the plane.

I have to mention too how much he was into sport. This quite surprised me at first, bearing in mind how incongruous his interest in, say, football was, compared to other aspects of his character. Whenever world cup level football was being televised he loved watching Brazil play with all their flair, passion and style. Freddie was also one of the best table tennis players I'd ever seen or played against. Where he learned, I don't know but he was phenomenal. At the studios, if there was a table, we'd always play, Freddie often abandoning his natural right hand and playing with his left, the other hand held behind his back.

His favourite non-active game was scrabble. He told me he'd been taught by an aunt as a child and he was a fanatical player. On tour, if he was playing when a sound check was due, he'd often miss the sound check rather than interrupt a game of scrabble that was becoming critical. He loved all word games, in fact. Recording abroad, he would always send me out every day to buy the English papers for the word games. I can see him punching the air in triumph when he successfully completed the word game in one paper.

Having just finished the 1992 Olympics, I'm reminded of the summer of 1976 when we watched the Montreal Olympics at The Manor Studios. Freddie was quite interested in that Olympiad. Although he never lived to see the Barcelona Olympics, that summer at The Manor could almost have been Freddie's last, making for an even more premature demise. One evening after dinner, Freddie announced that he wanted to return to London to see Mary who'd returned earlier with, I believe, an ear infection. There were no readily available cars returning to London that evening and the suggestion of me driving him in a transit van was greeted with one of his customary glares.

Finally, The Manor themselves offered the use of an estate car and with me driving, we set off to London. I felt the brakes as we left The Manor and thought they were a bit spongy but thought no more about the sponginess until, leaving the new M40 and joining the old A40, when braking as I approached one of the then numerous roundabouts, nothing happened when I pressed the pedal.

I managed to get about three quarters of the way round the traffic island before crashing into a huge pile of drainpipes, stacked ready for installation in nearby roadwork. As the car careered round, my only thought was the headline in the papers the following day:

"Roadie kills Pop Star!"

When the car came to rest, Freddie and I just looked at each other. We were completely unscathed; not a scratch.

After we'd got out of the car to survey the damage, some gypsies who were camped along the roadside came along and suggested we legged it immediately before the police arrived. Another couple of carloads of people stopped to make sure that no one was hurt and then went on. Freddie then decided to take control.

I shall never forget him standing there at the roadside. He hadn't shaved for two days, was wearing white clogs, blue jeans and a black silk Japanese kimono with something about *Queen* emblazoned on the back, a gift from a fan on the recent tour of Japan. Well, off he marched to someone's house at the roadside to find a telephone to ring for Derek, his usual driver, to come out from London and collect him. What the people in the house thought when we knocked on the door, I can only imagine but at least they recognised him. Yes, he could use the 'phone; would he like a cup of tea? Yes, he'd like a cup of tea. But... The meter had run out so off they went to borrow five pence coins; then there was no milk to put in the tea...

Finally Derek arrived and whisked Freddie off to London and the tow truck arrived to remove the battered car. Freddie had managed to ring The Manor and a great posse of people had set off, Roger in his Range Rover etc., expecting to find a mass of mangled metal. What did they find instead?

Me, sitting on my briefcase on the side of the A40 and not a thing to show for all the panic.

Although an off duty policeman was apparently one of the witnesses, no police action was taken against me because of the accident as it was indeed found that The Manor's estate car had defective brakes. However, it was a hairy moment and I heard Freddie later recalling the experience as he gave an interview in the music press when he announced to the interviewer that he certainly had experienced his life flashing in front of his eyes. He never laid any blame whatsoever at my door for that and in fact congratulated me for getting us out of the incident so lightly. I may add that I drove him countless times thereafter and he never displayed any worries about being my passenger. In some sneaking way and despite the potential seriousness of the accident, I also fancy he made a little mileage himself out of the drama of the affair.

GARY LANGHAN

During the recording of the last two tracks of *Sheer Heart Attack,* it was really the first time I'd been able to see how you could turn a control room into something it had never been. No longer were control rooms fixed and safe and rigid – I learned that anything that was required could be done, that the control room could be extended, added to and altered to provide whatever the band wanted. When a band moved in, it would become their home. A drinks trolley and fridges would materialise. The basic form was just taken over and worked over to provide the environment and effects that were required. We had every piece of equipment possible in there. I remember having two tape machines gaffer-taped to the control desk just to get one single phasing effect it would have been otherwise impossible to get with just the basic desk.

Having worked with *Queen* and Freddie, you just knew that every album was going to be wonderful. The moment I first remember knowing that was when we played the finally-put-together *Bo Rhap.* I stood at the back of the control room and just gasped. It was amazing.

There was a very touching and funny moment when Jill Sinclair's father who owned Sarm, burst into the studio one day to find Rag, Tag and Bobtail in the control room and yelled out: "So *you're* the Queen!" Mike went bright red and Freddie looked daggers at this old chap. Mike then managed to make a few introductions to smooth the situation over.

The only time that Fred was not at the control desk was when Brian was doing his guitar solos. Being even more of a perfectionist than Freddie at these times, it could take him days to perfect what he wanted.

In those early years, there was a great partnership between Roy Thomas Baker and Freddie. Sad that they parted but then like great partnerships, having made so many albums the emotional proximity had ultimately taken its toll.

Maybe people don't realise that the making of a record actually involves people being emotionally involved in the project from the beginning to the end. Freddie would take just as much care of where such and such a harmony was to go as he would in choosing the typeface and the colours used on the album cover. This sounds as though I'm being hard on the band but I'm sure that if you talked to them they would acknowledge that with Freddie at the helm, they trusted that nothing was going to be let slip. Freddie just got the best out of the rest of the band, he was always pushing them, making them strive for something different. They were always very proud of the fact they made good honest music, that nothing was faked up. From those studio roots, it was always acknowledged that everything they recorded could be done live, could be performed. Nothing was synthesised then; not until *Radio Gaga,* which was Roger's song, did *Queen* use anything synthesised.

CAUGHT IN THE LANDSLIDE

Freddie was always intensely supportive of other people's song-writing in the band and would give as much attention to one of the other's as he would to his own. It was so unlike other bands I've worked with where there is an acknowledged songwriter and anyone else who writes one really has a hassle to get it anywhere.

I remember one dreadful moment during the recording of *Death on Two Legs* when Freddie was doing the lead vocal. He was so incensed having worked himself into such an emotional state and the track in his headphones had become louder and louder. He took his cans off and suddenly there was blood pouring out of his ears. He was *so* angry. No one would ever believe how much hate and venom went into both the singing of that song let alone the lyrics themselves.

When they finally got some decent money after *Bo Rhap*, I remember Freddie had been out and bought up half of Harrods. He returned one afternoon after a huge spree in Christopher Wray's buying Tiffany lamps, saying:

"I'm tired, darling. I just can't *spend* any more money!"

Killer Queen was obviously a big step forward in the way of studio and recording techniques. It was Freddie, *Queen* and Roy which started all those staggeringly new developments which just took you off on an amazing journey. You never knew where it was going to land you. The songs didn't follow any of the strict formats that songs followed in those days.

I thought they were one of the hardest working bands. They were diligent and conscientious. There was a tremendous upside to working with all these people but I think it gave me a very odd perception of what the business was all about for there was nothing around which was remotely like *Queen* and Freddie. It was only when I started working with Trevor Horn that I found someone who was so careful and diligent, and prepared to go as far as it was necessary to go to make the best possible work of art. It's like two athletes, only one of whom is prepared and capable, I suppose, of going through the pain barrier. It was a bit of a blow to me, quite a disappointment to find out that after working with *Queen*, there were few bands who could match up to their standards.

Working with them was, I suppose, a matter of being born at the right time and coming into the studio at the right moment. It was Roy Thomas Baker who loved Sarm, the sound he knew he could achieve from the console and the control room. Roy had always previously worked at Trident where he was the house sound engineer.

The reception for *A Night At The Opera* was at the White Elephant on the River. I walked in and there were *Queen* holding up a huge telegram from Groucho Marx. Freddie really adored the Marx Brothers and it was such a great moment for him to get the telegram. He loved the acknowledgement and reciprocated by sending Groucho platinum albums.

CHRIS TAYLOR

At the end of the 1976 world tour, we went off to Ridge Farm to rehearse *A Day At The Races*. Then we went to the Manor Studios to record it. As we were all living and working in the same building, it was the first time we realised that they were all human beings and had a sense of humour.

The point of all our lives was simply enjoying ourselves and we lived life from hangover to hangover. We were all glad when we saw thirty.

The first time I realised about Fred's sense of humour though was really in 1979 when we were recording the *Live Killers* album on tour in Europe. Fred and Brian would sing *Love of my Life*. I had to walk on stage with a pair of maracas and a glass of water to give to Fred. One night, at the end of the previous song, Fred started bowing in his harlequin leotard very theatrically and I start walking on with the maracas and the water. Then he starts bowing again and I step back. Then he stops and I start coming again. He finally takes the water and the maracas from me and then announces to twelve thousand people:

"This is Crystal and I hear he's got a big c..k and he's good in bed!"

I legged it and whispered: "I'm never doing that again!"

From that moment on, everyone on the tour took it in turns to take on the maracas and the water, like one night it was the chef, the next it was John Etchells, covered from head to foot in recording tape as he was recording the album in the mobile studio. On another night it was Joe Travato's turn, the lighting designer. When Freddie saw Joe walk on he exclaimed:

"You're supposed to be doing my lights! You're fired, you c..t!" Then he laughed.

On the very last night of the tour, just for the hell of it, I made a final guest appearance with about twenty pairs of maracas taped together like a bunch of flowers and presented them to Freddie.

Once we got to Munich, recording *The Game* album, it was then we became once and for all what Fred called 'the family'. We became all very very close. Each day we would go into the studio and about six o'clock every night, Jobbie, Brian's guitar roadie, would start making cocktails. Then it would be dinner and drinks and, later, out clubbing. Everybody used to go to the Sugar Shack except Freddie and Phoebe (Peter Freestone) who'd go to some 'ginge' club as Freddie would call them, like Mrs. Henderson's. At the end of the night we would all meet up in Roger's and my suite, the HH – the Hetero Hangout - or Freddie and Phoebe's suite which was called the PPP – The Presidential Pouff Parlour – and get even more 'out of it'.

It was round about that time that I started travelling with the band instead of the crew and I got to know Freddie much better. We became very close and I became one of the very privileged few who was able to go and knock on his door any time of day or night. Some people even thought we were having an affair!

I've used the word 'family' a lot but it really was like that. We were self-sufficient in every way. We'd come off tour after six months and you'd think we'd all be sick of the sight of each other, but within a couple of days we'd all be on the 'phone to each other and then round at Fred's gaff, playing Trivial Pursuit 'til some unearthly hour.

On the last day of the tour before Knebworth we were in Marbella, at the Marbella Club. Roger and I had a villa together and Freddie and Straker had the one next door. Roger and I got out of our minds and I, for some unknown reason, couldn't sleep and so I took a couple of Valium! Freddie and Straker came back to their villa and Fred decided he wanted to talk to me. Straker rang the wrong Taylor and woke Roger up instead of me. The next thing I know I wake up out of a drugged sleep with Freddie at the foot of my bed saying:

"Come on, come on, wake up. I want to talk to you. You do this to me all the time, now it's my turn."

While I was groping around the room for a robe, he grabbed me by the arm and said:

"Now learn to play an instrument, you c..t. You're in the band now!"

I knew it was going to be a rough few hours but somehow I managed to wake up...

Freddie and Monserrat were due to perform *Barcelona* at a huge concert in Barcelona in front of the King and Queen of Spain and a hundred and thirty thousand Spaniards to promote Barcelona's staging of the 1992 Olympic Games. Jerry Lee Lewis, Jose Carreras who did a duet with Dionne Warwick, *Spandau Ballet*, lots of opera singers, Eddie Grant. It was a spectacular bill. By that time, I'd left *Queen* and I'd gone out there with Mike Moran to help put together the backing band for the show.

When Fred found out I was there I was summoned to Fred's suite. I took Hobson who worked for *Spandau* up to meet Fred, and Hobson was a bit nervous of meeting such a mega-star. After we'd been there some time, Fred turned to Hobson and said:

"Who are you?"

Hobson replied that he did drums for Spandau Ballet. Freddie said:

"What's her name? What's she called, the drummer?"

"John Keeble," Hobson replied.

"That's right. Keeble, Keyball, Keyboards." Then a pause.

"Keyboards, keyboards... What do you mean. I thought you said you did drums!"

Hobson was very confused by this time but then it was eight o'clock in the morning and we had "gone to Neptune on a Magic Swan". Just before we left, Freddie threw open the hotel window, flung his arms into the air and yelled:

"Barcelona, I am here... At last we are at one!"

It's ironic that it was Fred's last live public performance and things f...ed up. Nobody else realised, but to him it was a disaster. The backing tape that he and Montserrat were singing to was running slow throughout and Fred was not amused, to say the least. I can honestly say I had no idea what was happening but because Freddie had written and produced it and was extremely close to it, he was obviously aware that it was running a smidge slow!

I know that this is all about Freddie but I have to say that the other three guys in *Queen* played an equally important role in the band's, and therefore Freddie's, success. As far as I'm concerned, they were always a unit right to the end. Even though they argued amongst themselves, heaven forbid that an outsider said anything about 'the family'. Just like marriage, a few squabbles during the day but then a f...ing good time at night!

BILLY SQUIER

Freddie was not an easy person to get to. At first, I thought him kind of aloof. He obviously had a good defence system in place around him although I never got the impression that this was a contrived thing. It seemed natural but nonetheless said 'Private' in no uncertain terms. You knew you'd have to wait to be let in – but you didn't mind waiting around for the invitation.

I felt he was very sensitive and yet at the same time very strong – in fact, because he was always so positive and affirmative, he seemed to be fearless. Logic said that there surely had to be an area inside of him which wasn't quite that sure but it wasn't until I worked with him that I even glimpsed this vulnerable side to him.

He always put himself, professionally, at tremendous risk and would go to any lengths to take those risks, so much so that many must have thought him, at times, the fool rushing in where angels proverbially feared to tread. It's very lonely taking those steps for, in the end, few – if any – go with you. It's what I call the pyramid theory; the higher you climb towards the pinnacle, the less room there is for other people on the ledge beside you and certainly, when you stand on the very apex, you're in your own unique company. That was his dilemma.

Sure, people will watch you as you go up that pyramid but essentially it is *your* struggle. You have to have great belief in yourself to be able to live like he did.

I saw from close-hand just how forceful he could be. I supported *Queen* on their last tour of the USA and performed with him when he sang *Jailhouse Rock* and songs like that. He loved to perform. I think all the words about how great a performer he was have been used up. I just used to stand and watch him every night thinking: *"How* do you *do* that? Just *how* do you get away with it?"* It was the on-stage Freddie that was most fearless. He believed in what he and the band were doing so much, he never projected the slightest fear or self-doubt and that just swept the audience along with him. He just *knew* that the show was going to work. He was made for the stage. His sense of theatricality was the key and it was a key which so very few other rock performers have at their disposal.

I learned tremendously from his self-confidence. He taught me a lot about believing in myself. When we worked together, there were a lot of things I would have shied away from doing had he not pushed me into trying.

At one stage, I was doing an album in England for Capitol, a record label he and I shared in common. With Ratty, (Peter Hince), who was helping me out over the recording period, I went over to Logan Place to see him. I very much wanted to see the house he was so proud of and which he'd taken so many years to get just so. It was great to see him again and he lost no time in asking to hear what I'd been working on after several years of moving in different directions. I started playing him some roughs and he got incredibly enthused. He would make me play songs over and over again, always interjecting ideas, playing 'air guitar'. We eventually managed to stay up the entire night.

At about ten o'clock the following morning, he suddenly announced that he'd "got an idea for that song, dear. What's it called?"

"You mean Love is the Hero?" I asked. He went downstairs and sat at his piano. It was one of those misty London mornings, the light filtering gently in through that huge window of the piano room at Logan Place. As though it came from nowhere, he just sat down and played the most perfect introduction to my song. I was amazed how easily the composition flowed out. Later, he recorded it properly at the studio, improving it in some subtly different way at each take. He kept doing it over and over until it was perfect, not at all self-conscious about the time he was taking or the experimental directions he'd pursue and then abandon.

We later started working on another song he had taken a fancy to. He'd said that he didn't think the lyrics I had were interesting enough and didn't like the title. Again, from out of nowhere, he suddenly suggested it should be called Lady With a Tenor Sax; I had no idea what he had in mind but I'd learned by now that when Freddie had an idea it was generally best to go with it.

"Okay," I said, "but you'll have to write some lyrics 'cause at the moment I don't know where you're coming from."

At the studio, without any hesitation, he began singing... and the words came, like they were coming out of the ether – no preparation and very apt. (I later tried to develop this faculty in myself after seeing Freddie do it so successfully). He believed entirely where he was going – even if he didn't always know just where he was going and that's the key to writing spontaneously – you have to believe implicitly in what comes out.

When Lady... was finished, I assumed that his rough vocals would in fact make up the body of the recording and thought they were spectacular!. He insisted the opposite, that I would be much better singing it than him. I couldn't see this and was somewhat reluctant to try. He kept on and on, eventually bullying me into sing it myself. And, you know something? He was right. I somehow rose to the occasion and upon listening back we both agreed that my performance was 'the one'. I couldn't believe that I was actually up on this guy's level. That experience forced me to re-evaluate my perception of myself, made me realize that I should not be as reticent in taking up personal challenges and could be what I wanted to be... if only I believed.

Freddie was one of those writers who also wrote very much with performance in mind. Sometimes his lyrics would be entirely geared to his singing them in performance – in a Queen concert situation, lyrics which if sung by another artist would sound banal and mediocre.

Freddie was a labyrinthine personality, an endless series of rooms

111

each containing a different characteristic. He would rehearse and rehearse, yet end up doing something completely spontaneous. He was a perfectionist and yet would allow himself to take huge risks. I can't help thinking that it was these very opposites which created the dynamic of his unique persona.

TONY HADLEY

Singers, generally speaking, always go through kind of confidence crises. One minute you're up, one you're down. In the early days, my voice was a constant worry. Talking, as singers do about their voices, to Freddie, he told me:

"Darling! When they come to your concert, they come to see you. If you can't hit a note for some reason, don't worry. Just get on with it and relax and realise your strength and power as a performer!"

That was some time ago but I took that advice to heart and I think it was probably the best advice I've ever had from anyone in the business.

Spandau was on a world tour 1984 or '85. We were in Australia. While we were in Australia, we had some days off before going on to America. I'd heard that *Queen* were performing in New Zealand and so off I went with a minder, on the plane to see them. *Spandau* had cancelled their New Zealand tour for some reason and so I was advised to keep a low profile when I got there.

I arrived backstage in this big tent *Queen* had had built behind the huge open air stadium where they were playing. Freddie and I met up and went back to the hotel before the gig and sat at the bar, gradually drinking our way through a couple of bottles of Stolichnaya.

"Darling," he said when we were very pissed, "come up to the room, I've got a bottle of port up there. We're going to drink port!"

So up to the room we went and demolished the port as well as the Stolichnaya.

Then he insisted that I go on-stage with them that night. Roger and John were told and Brian was soon in on the act too. We didn't know what to sing and Freddie suggested *Jailhouse Rock*.

"But I don't know the words," I protested.

"Nor do I, darling!" he replied.

We then tried, between the two of us, to work out the words for *Jailhouse Rock*, at least words that made sense. We wrote them down and agreed that he would sing the first line and me the second. At least, that was the plan.

On-stage they go, with me waiting in the wings. The piano was on my side of the stage and at one point Freddie ended up in his performance straddled across the piano, staring at me and shouting:

"Hadley, you bastard! You've got me so pissed!"

Freddie announced that I was coming on-stage and on I strode. *Jailhouse Rock* starts but we both end up abandoning the plan and making up the words all over again as we go along. Freddie was probably truer to the original plan than me but who's to say. The rest of *Queen* were looking at us as though we were crazy! Still, we got through it and the crowd loved it.

Back at the hotel afterwards, there's tons of messages from Steve Dagger my manager who finally gets through to tell me to remember to keep a *very* low profile in New Zealand. I came clean as there wasn't anything I could do about it, having just been on-stage in front of 45,000 people.

I went upstairs to see Freddie who was propped up in bed in silk sheets and things and unable to come down to the party, more to do with the amount of alcohol he'd consumed rather than any stage strain.

"Tonight?," he said blearily, "No way, darling. I've got gigs to do, tours to do... "

That moment of going on-stage with Freddie and the boys is up there in my memory along with *Live Aid* and all those massive concerts I've done. The opportunity comes along so rarely that it's a once in a lifetime thing. The memory of it will never fade.

If he thought that what you were doing had potential and was musically interesting and that you were going far, he would give his time and energy to what you were doing and look out for you in future. He had nothing to gain from all that but I think it was a respectful thing he wanted to do for the generation that was coming up behind him.

DIANA MOSELEY

Born to Love You was in 1985. I did another three videos after that in that year.

The following year I was asked to help out on the European Tour which meant doing all the jackets with the little buckles on and the cloaks for Freddie. You had to be gentle with *Queen*; Brian needed a little coaxing. You couldn't just rush in and push things too far. After the first technical runs in Sweden, I got a call from Freddie who thought it wasn't really working and the show needed a lift. He'd decided that at the end of the show he wanted to come out and take his final bows in an ermine gown and a crown. He wanted me to get the costume ready for Paris.

The metal crown and the ermine gown were finished and Jim Beach called me to tell me to take the stuff to Paris myself. There I was with Jim and Roxy Mead, the PR, in the limo going to Heathrow airport with a giant metal crown in a cardboard box, the top sticking out of the box's flaps. The crown set off every possible alarm system on the security network but we eventually arrived, the crown intact except for the tip.

The crown fitting was going to be somewhat nerve-racking and beforehand we had tea; lots of little sandwiches and cakes. Freddie emerged from his suite in his yellow tracksuit.

"Where's the crown, dear?" he called with his mouth full of cucumber sandwich.

He grabbed the box, whipped out the crown and stuck it on his head and... it fitted! Thank God.

He spent the rest of the afternoon wearing the crown *and* the cloak, practising the wearing of the ensemble for later. He sashayed around the hotel suite rehearsing his walk and then asked Crystal for his mike... No mike being available, he substituted a banana and in this full regalia, swept out into the corridor of the hotel and along the landing, creating a royal show for the entire hotel.

Later, on the way to the concert, I was standing quite close to him in the foyer as he waited to leave the hotel in the motorcade with the police outriders. He was already flexing himself for the performance and as he was about to go through the doors and face the battery of television cameras and press reporters, I heard him murmur to himself:

"Right! As soon as I'm out of that door, I'm theirs."

It was a magical moment, that sudden transformation of the private man into public property.

That was his job.

TREVOR CLARKE

There are so many stories I have to tell about Freddie. His generosity; of course! He was responsible for so many memorable trips I've made to Boston and New York to see the band in concert. Madison Square Garden was wonderful. Fabulous parties – the one in Ibiza was very memorable. On the flight over, Anita Dobson and I swapped uniforms with the crew to serve champagne to our fellow passengers, some of whom were behaving a little too stiffly, we decided!

But it's easy to be generous when you have a lot of money. What it's not easy being is thoughtful when you're so famous and have so many calls on your time. That's something that can only be quantified by experience and so here are two experiences of mine when I've had the deepest reasons to be grateful for Freddie's thoughtfulness.

In 1978, I was still working at Maunkberry's and we were faced with a new club opening in competition; The Embassy in Bond Street. The night in question was the opening night of this new club and although I had of course been invited, I was desperate to go along to sum up the competition.

I was getting ready in the afternoon when I had a sudden premonition, the sort that leaves you cold like you've been touched by some freezing cold force. I instantly thought of my mother at home in Stoke Newington and immediately telephoned my sister at work and asked her to go home at once. As I was finishing off at home before leaving for this grand opening, I had a telephone call from my nephew, my sister's child:

"Uncle Trevor, Uncle Trevor, I can't wake granny!"

I told the child gently to go next door and wait with the lady there until my sister, his mother, came over.

I knew it then. My mother was dead.

I raced across London and after arranging for the doctor to come, the undertaker to call and remove my mother's body, I hurried back to Bond Street and somehow got through the evening. Nightclub work is notoriously social and being social when your heart is so heavy was no easy task.

I must have told some people about my loss – my cousin Rudi for one – and people were very kind. By the end of the evening I was back at Maunkberry's thinking out how to put into action some urgent changes which I knew we would have to make after seeing how successful the Embassy Club was going to be.

There was a 'phone call. It was Freddie:

"I've heard, dear. You're not to go back to your place. Come here. Come and stay here. At least for tonight. The car's waiting for you outside."

It was a life-saver, the ultimate gesture of sympathy and affection when I needed it most. I really loved my mother and felt very alone now that she had gone. That night, Freddie put his arm round me and said:

"Don't worry, dear. I'm your mother now."

From then on, whenever he called he would say:

"Hello, dear. Mother here."

From that day, he always had me over to the house on Christmas day and every year arranged a little party to celebrate my birthday with a few close friends. Until he died.

Later, much later I was working in the banqueting department of a big London hotel where I contracted what turned out to be a very dangerous case of food poisoning in the middle of a very grand celebration being given by one of the Rothschild family. For obvious reasons, I can't mention the hotel!

Somehow, I got myself home in a taxi and spent the next few days in bed. I went to one doctor who prescribed panadol! I'd spoken to Freddie and the boys at Logan Place obviously but they had no reason to suspect that I wouldn't be up and about in twenty four hours. A couple of friends and family came round but when you live by yourself, you're often more on your own than you think and if you're ill, it can be very frightening.

I didn't realise how dehydrated I was becoming but after I began passing blood, I telephoned Freddie's household again as in terms of proximity, they were my closest friends. Very weakly, I started explaining what was happening to me. Freddie grabbed the telephone, told me to stay put, that he was sending his own doctor round straightaway and that no expense would be spared to get me well again as quickly as possible. He even took care of all the catering and ordered food and drink and supplies to be sent round to my flat immediately.

In a few hours, my four rooms were loaded with enough stuff to feed a fair-sized third world country and, of course, I recovered.

SARAH HARRISON

It's so hard to try and pinpoint the high spots of my friendship with Freddie. There were so many.

As I mentioned, I met Freddie whilst working as Cat Stevens' personal assistant. Working for anyone in the music business is very demanding on both time and energy but since all my friends in those days were in similarly demanding jobs in the same business, work and play definitely overlapped. We were a very close-knit group of people and, naturally, socialising was very much part of this completely overlapping private and professional life we lived.

When socialising with Freddie, however, things were always very much under *his* control.

I remember one night going with Freddie and a group of friends, all male, to the discotheque Heaven only for the club to refuse us entry. No girls were allowed. Freddie immediately came to the fore.

"Now come along, dear," he said to the doorman, "It's very simple... You either let us all in or none of us will come in." Faced with this ultimatum, of course the guy had no alternative and I was the only girl in Heaven that night!

My friendship with Freddie took on another facet when in 1976 I went to work as personal assistant to Harvey Goldsmith, the concert promoter. In those days of course, Harvey promoted every band which was worth promoting – still does as a matter of fact – so naturally, I found myself working with *Queen* and *Queen* really meant Freddie. Since Freddie didn't socialise much with the others in the band with the exception of Roger, I hadn't met all of them before working with them but there is no doubt that knowing Freddie gave me an inbuilt advantage.

One of the first gigs I remember was in Liverpool where I was charged with looking after the band because Harvey was unable to be there. I had the problem of finding a restaurant which would not only take a booking for this motley crew at the necessarily late hour after their show but a restaurant which would satisfy Freddie's rather discerning palate and this was all apart from the further problem of trying to find a club for the band to go onto afterwards! Thinking back, I have a vague memory of ending up in the Penthouse restaurant of the Post House Hotel!

Soon enough, of course, the band's gigs progressed to Wembley Arena, Wembley Stadium and Earl's Court and the problem of finding restaurants became somewhat simpler.

Everything was fun and very spontaneous around Freddie. I remember one evening at Country Cousin when *Queen* were about to do a major concert at Madison Square Garden in New York. The band had just released *The News of the World* album and the twin anthems of *We Are The Champions* and *We Will Rock You* were sweeping the world. John Reid, *Queen*'s manager, went round all of us at the table promising us a trip on the new Freddie Laker Skytrain to New York to see the show. Although Freddie and the band were the toast of New York, Freddie was thrilled to see all of us. This extravagant gesture on John's part very much sums up the way of our lives at that time.

At the same time that *Queen* were rising to their super-stardom, Freddie demonstrated his ability to maintain his close friendships. We were all well-trusted with the facts of his private life and although Freddie never made any attempt to hide any part of his nature, the fact that he was at the same time a very private person made it a very special privilege to be a part of that inner circle of closed friends.

He was the most generous of people. In fact, his friends were treated just as his family, with Christmas and birthdays being made much of. Of course, present giving was always a problem when giving to Freddie was concerned although what a pleasure it was when you knew you had made the right choice of something for him. It didn't make you feel as reticent about opening those lovely red Cartier boxes!

Freddie was a great host and a terrific party giver. I was one of the guests at the fantastic extravaganza given at Country Cousin for his thirtieth birthday and it really was a spectacular evening. Freddie loved to have a good time and he always wanted everyone else to have a good time too. And there were countless good times, in clubs, in restaurants, at his home, at concerts, at the ballet and the opera... Freddie was always up-to-date with the newest ballet stars and I remember seeing Mikhail Baryshnikov's first performance at Covent Garden with Freddie who, of course, led the rousing applause.

After he bought his house in Logan Place, Freddie could indulge his taste for extravagance. I remember being totally floored when I realised that one of the forty feet high side windows in the house were curtained with nothing less than Fortuny fabric!

Logan Place was also the scene of the famous Hat Party. No one was allowed in without the necessary headgear and the party lasted from mid-afternoon into the early hours of the following day.

Another even more extravagant party was held on the island of Ibiza. Freddie arranged for a whole plane-load of us to be flown out there for the party which was held at Pikes Hotel. I think Freddie must have thought our group perhaps a little staid because he ended up by inviting all the boys and girls from the 'hottest' clubs in the nearby towns and these turned up in droves to add a certain something to the evening. Needless to say, a great time was had by all, with the addition of flamenco dancers, people in fancy dress not to mention Wayne Sleep pirouetting around the pool which was of course graced by the presence of several fully clothed guests during the course of the evening. Although Freddie wasn't very much in evidence that night – I think he was also recording with Montserrat Caballé – his was nevertheless the presence which had brought everyone together and it illustrates his very catholic taste in people!

Despite his deep love of fun and outrageous sense of humour coupled with his love to shock, Freddie was a thoroughly professional musician and worked hard to make sure that *Queen* were always on top of their form. For many people, whatever their taste in music, *Queen* were the ultimate live band and it was to a large extent Freddie's showmanship, charisma and talent which helped to make the band such a success. It's no mean task, either, to hold together a rather disparate group of people for twenty years and for their last album together to be arguably their best ever.

NIGEL QUINEY

After our first meeting, I went to Freddie's house for parties or lunches several times as indeed did he come to mine.

His house fascinated me in that the main sitting room had once been an artist's studio and had enormous height and space. It was full of varied collections of objets although for me the pieces of glass from Daum and by Lalique were especially exciting. They were exactly the type I loved, big statements, chunky and not over decorated. Elsewhere, were more elaborate examples of Freddie's taste and I loved his ability and confidence to mix these varied styles. There were many pieces of chinoiserie, art nouveau and ormolu along with huge overstuffed settees and armchairs surrounding thick, heavy glass tables, objets placed on the tables along with sweetmeats and cigarettes. Of course there was the huge piano with dozens of silver photograph frames on it. It was a very opulent setting. Cristal champagne seemed forever on tap, served in a variety of lovely glasses which I would always have been rather nervous of breaking had they been mine.

I never saw anything of the sex, drugs and rock 'n' roll which as a newcomer to this fabled scene I had been keeping half an eye open for. Freddie would move around his guests with the ease of a natural host, displaying an elegance yet at the same time exuding a strange mixture of macho and camp. He was obviously very proud of his house and his collections. I could not help remarking on the individuality of his style which he had brought to this very unusual Edwardian wealthy artist's domain. Clearly, if he couldn't find what he was looking for in the way of furniture, he designed his own and had it made. Here, his non-European background would express itself and yet the unusual pieces he collected and created somehow fitted in to effect a balanced whole.

I always felt his colour sense was so unusual. It was not my own taste but I was always fascinated by the colours he put together. I suppose I'm trying to say that Freddie was truly unique. You knew that he didn't scour the pages of the *House and Garden* magazine for his ideas.

And then there were the cats... Cats are my favourite animals and Freddie's almost seemed to be everywhere, rubbing their cheeks against the legs of the chair, slinking round the side of the sofa, padding across a fabulous rug to leap effortlessly onto the top of the piano. They would have given me a heart attack when I think how they picked their way elegantly through the forest of fragile treasures. I asked Freddie if much got broken. Strangely, I can't remember his reply but clearly the cats were more important than anything that might have been toppled and broken. He adored them and they were indeed adorable.

What surprised me most of all as I got to know him better was how easy he was to be with. He was genuinely interested in so many things and he had that lovely curiosity which makes for such natural conversation. An early conversation was about school days and their effect upon our lives. I had personally hated mine; clearly this was not the case for Freddie. I was amazed that he had such a vivid memory for individual boys from school days. My memory, with one exception, was almost blank. Gosh. I thought, a pop star still remembers that far back...

He had had the same absolute fascination with movies that I had seen as a teenager. The larger than life images projected by Hollywood in glorious Cinemascope and Technicolour had affected Freddie in the same way as they had affected me. A great game was testing the memory to see who could remember the names of obscure movie queens from yesteryear and their films. This always led to... "And what d'you think they're doing now?". Shades of Veronica Lake and Hedy Lamarr were always summoned up, serving customers from behind the counters of downtown Los Angeles department stores. I don't think for a moment that Freddie ever saw himself suddenly being penniless and serving behind the sock counter at Harrods but he was always aware of the frailty of fame. He also inherited from those early days of picture going a great instinct for the power of things theatrical. His videos illustrate his observation and as I watch them I always think of that teenage boy avidly haunting his local cinema during his school holidays in Zanzibar whilst I was doing exactly the same thing half way across the world at the Granada, Tooting.

It must be quite obvious that I am not an avid aficionado of pop music; my record collection stops with Tamla Motown in its demise. Thus does age catch up. My friendship with Freddie was therefore not based at all on my being knowledgeable about his music and career. In my own work, I travel extensively and it was on one of my long haul trips that I finally realised Freddie's world class stature. After leaving a factory in the jungles of Malaysia, I settled in the back of the car for a two hour journey to Kuala Lumpur. We were driving through an incredible tropical storm and you could see little through the windows of the car. I was tired and put my head back and relaxed. The music from the speakers behind me quietly permeated my conscious state. Ah! One of my great favourites from my teenage was being played. *The Great Pretender*. It had had great meaning at that time in my life. But... Something was wrong. It wasn't *The Platters* singing. Strange, I thought. The voice, however, seemed familiar. At first I was irritated but suddenly realised I liked this unfamiliar interpretation. I closed my eyes and then of course I realised it was Freddie. I was amazed as I never thought he sang those old songs.

I asked my host, a young Malaysian businessman skilled in the manufacture of plastic trash bags if he knew who was singing. The reply was immediate.

"Sure! That's Freddie Mercury!".

I felt so proud.

CHERRY BROWN

I have to mention that the words of *We are the champions* were written in the kitchen of my flat in St. Edmund's Terrace only to set the scene for my first experience of real stardom at close quarters.

Freddie had 'borrowed' my flat for an evening and the following day, after we'd had a very jolly breakfast, he got on the telephone and ordered up his chauffeured car which then whisked he and I off to Harrods. The chauffeur who also acted as bodyguard accompanied us through the store to the perfume department where Freddie, having ascertained my taste in fragrances, proceeded to buy me the biggest bottle of L'Air du Temps that I had ever seen. It bore the most colossal price tag and I remember thinking in my impecunious state that it could have probably have bought me a fairly decent house! However, despite the feeble remonstrations of my conscience, I ultimately had no intention of refusing such a wonderful present.

However, Freddie was soon spotted. The atmosphere in Harrods' perfume department turned from sedate select calm to major panic and flurry. Suddenly, I turned and Freddie was gone. Derek, his driver, whisked him almost invisibly out and away and I was left holding my huge bottle of L'Air du Temps completely alone!

I remember many wonderful moments at Country Cousin too. The most memorable as far as Freddie was concerned was when Hebe, a seasoned cabaret performer, a woman only slightly less outrageous than Freddie himself, was performing part of her act standing on the long refectory table which was set down the middle of the restaurant. As she parted the way before her, gently pushing people's plates an glasses aside with her feet, she found herself standing above the celebrated Mr. Mercury.

Of course everyone was glued to the sight. Freddie's eyes suddenly seemed equally glued to the floor but Hebe did not relent and in the manner of a dotty schoolmistress encouraged, coaxed and finally forced – "Up! Come on! Up, up!" – poor Freddie to his feet and from thence to join her at the table where, very bravely, he finally cast his acute embarrassment and seething reluctance aside and sang *God Save The Queen* in wonderfully outrageous manner as Hebe conducted him with her fan!

You see, he *was* a very quiet person. I really don't think he was shy as such but he was... quiet. To see him turn into this unbelievable showman was amazing to me. Suddenly, there was this flamboyant performer, the ultimate performer as far as I was concerned. But it only held true in specific situations. In concert halls, stadiums... places like that. Put Freddie in front of 70,000 fans, he was limitless. In front of a roomful of a hundred and fifty people, he would never have even thought of getting up and singing *God Save The Queen*.

He became a very accessible star, I felt. Whenever a *Queen* album came out, he would never fail to see me and sign the copy I'd bought for my nephew Christopher and I shall always remember him sitting on my sofa when he came over and having deep and loving conversations with my dog, Scarlet, a delicate and ladylike red setter. He was just as potty about his cats.

ELAINE PAIGE

I'd known Freddie socially since 1986. He loved to entertain and I was often invited to his house parties. One day I approached him to discuss an idea of recording an orchestral album of Queen's music. His reaction was amazing; he literally jumped up and down.

"Darling, marvellous! Marvellous!"

He was absolutely thrilled at the idea of hearing his music interpreted in a new way. So, The *Queen* Album began to take shape.

During the recording sessions, Mike Moran, the producer, and I had only been in the studio a short while before Freddie came down. As always he was very enthusiastic and very supportive. We had worked on just two tracks, one of which was *Bohemian Rhapsody* and he was amazed at the way it all sounded as indeed we all were when played by the New Philharmonic, a huge orchestra. He just loved it.

We then played him *It's A Kind Of Magic.* It was at this point that Freddie could stand it no longer. He leapt out of his seat in the control room, charged into the studio and began readjusting my microphone for his *own* use! He ended up of course by singing through the whole of *It's A Kind Of Magic* but what he hadn't realise was that the song had been transposed into my key so poor Freddie was screeching away in a key far too high for him but loving every second of it.

Freddie was one of the most responsive and talented people I've ever met. Creativity just poured out of him. He was so involved with my recording that he practically forgot to return to Montreux where he was recording the *Miracle* Album with *Queen.* In fact, we all met up there later on for a playback of his new album which turned into a crazy weekend of music, wining and dining somewhere half way up a mountain!

During this time our relationship developed and he became a great friend, always turning up the first nights of my shows and my concerts. His advice was invaluable as it was always constructive, honest and to the point.

JAMES ARTHURS

By late 1976, I'd moved into Central Manhattan just a few blocks away from the Waldorf Astoria. I'd been transferred to the headquarters of my company in Rockefeller Centre in the RCA Building where I held a senior position in the international division. Little did I know at the time that not only was this move good for my career but it resulted in the blossoming of my friendship with Freddie. A Jekyll and Hyde existence ensued of business by day and frequent rock 'n' roll by night and at weekends. Freddie always wondered how I managed to stay up all night and work all day when he was in town. But, when he started to use my apartment as a hideaway when he was on private visits to New York, he found out my secret which was that I took two hour naps here and there between work and before going out to dinner and the late visits to the clubs and bars. I also used to crash out completely once he'd left town and in those days he rarely stayed more than a week even when doing concerts.

Freddie didn't know New York too well back then and so my apartment became a small oasis in the caravan of events, a place to just drop and relax if only for a few hours. He'd call me up a few days before arriving whether he was going to stay in a hotel or with me. The conversation always ended with roughly the same line: "... and darling, please see if you can't find a nice new restaurant and a few interesting bars!" So, I'd ask around and check out the places and I'd be ready for Freddie!

My location was so convenient when he was in town that normally, even when he stayed at the Waldorf Astoria or another hotel nearby, our friends visiting from England would often stay with me resulting in a constant to-and-fro between my apartment and the hotel with a limousine almost continuously outside the entrance to one or the other place. The evenings became more and more fun, sometimes verging on the outrageous. We became a regular little gang, piling into one or two limos depending on our numbers and then driving off into the night to thoroughly explore Manhattan from central Park to Greenwich village, 'Studio 54' to 'One Fifth' followed only by even more revelries in the early morning back at the hotel. When visiting the clubs and bars, Freddie would have the driver stop the limo some fifty to a hundred yards away from the entrance of whichever club or bar we were going to so that we should not be conspicuous and we'd walk the rest of the way. On one occasion, a passer-by called out: "I see you know where it's at, Freddie!" as we strolled towards a bar, Freddie vainly attempting to be incognito. "Research, darling!" Freddie called back, "Research!"

I probably went to everyone of Freddie's New York concerts over the next four years until I moved out of Manhattan once again. Our antiquing forays continued unabated, however, and I found myself eventually buying Japanese prints on his behalf at the New York

Sotheby's auctions. He'd call me from wherever he was and, at either end of the telephone line, we'd each have copies of the catalogue and he'd go through it, telling me the few lots he was interested in and the price he was prepared to go to. Occasionally he would abandon caution: "I have to have it. Pay anything, dear but get it! Only check the condition of it first!" Freddie only ever wanted the best.

I was visiting with him in Munich on one occasion in 1979. He was there with the other *Queen* members rehearsing somewhere nearby. We were sitting around in his hotel suite in the early evening slowly dragging ourselves together to go to dinner. Freddie went off for a bath but we suddenly heard him shouting: "Bring me the tape player - Quick!" The errand done, he later emerged from the bathroom humming. He sat down and played a few bars on the piano and then on the guitar.

We went off to a Vietnamese restaurant for dinner and then had a drink in a few bars but he was preoccupied the whole time, humming and then singing softly to himself.

By the end of the evening, back at the hotel, he was on the guitar again playing, finally, what was going to be *Queen*'s next massive hit, *Crazy Little Thing Called Love*. It was fascinating to be there while he was composing it and even more fascinating later to hear critics' comments that the song was a remake of an old hit by Elvis, Bill Haley or 'someone like that'.

Over the next few years, I met up with Freddie in Germany, Australia and Japan. Either it would be me visiting whilst on business trips or him although our business lives were far removed from each other. I went to his concerts and joined in what had became his standard after-hours carousing.

In Japan, we went to a dinner reception at 'Serena', a top Tokyo restaurant after *Queen*'s concert there. Freddie had some friends from Australia visiting him and I took a business colleague along. We were a group of about eight plus the rest of *Queen* and the road crew as well as the sedate and polite Japanese record company executives. It was a fun evening, Freddie becoming progressively wilder. As fruit was brought around for dessert, he exclaimed: "None here, darling! There's enough fruits here already!"

But beneath the veneer of all the fun and the superstar outrageousness, Freddie was vulnerable. He was sincere too and very thoughtful. He stayed very loyal to an inner group of friends, those who weren't just the temporary hangers-on who got bored in the quieter or off moments.

PETER FREESTONE

Three weeks after the Royal Opera House Gala, *Queen* were due to begin the *CRAZY* tour of England, playing only those small venues in which they had started out.

My boss at the Opera House, Michael Brown, had been telephoned by Paul Prenter from the *Queen* Office and asked to enquire whether there was anyone in the wardrobe who would be interested in supervising the costumes for all four members of *Queen* on the tour. At this point I have to explain that a career and therefore promotion at the Opera House was based on length of service and someone else in front of you dying! To leave the system of what was after all an institution for something as tempting but as flighty and as short term as a six week tour with even a top-flight rock band of the likes of *Queen* was almost unthinkable. To have done so would have meant that you would not be able to waltz back into the Opera House system again because someone else's foot would be on your rung of the promotion ladder.

It should go without saying that when Michael Brown asked us if there was anyone who wanted to take up Paul Prenter's offer, my hand went up immediately!

Had I stayed at the Opera House, now, twenty years later, I *might* just have been assistant Wardrobe Master. *Just.* I suppose I have to acknowledge a shamelessly pragmatic approach to my career but then I've only ever had four jobs in my life and so I can't have been that foolish.

It was the time of *Queen* writing for the *Flash Gordon* movie directed by Mike Hodges and the band were rehearsing for the tour at Shepperton Film Studios where indeed they often had rehearsed. I arrived on the duly appointed day and Paul Prenter told me to go off and look through the costumes. People were milling around everywhere, roadies, technical staff, drivers, assistants and ... well, everyone looked so much the same that when Paul Prenter introduced me to the other members of *Queen* I honestly hadn't realised who they were. In rehearsals the band displayed no crowing attitudes whatsoever. The only person I *had* noticed was Jim Beach, their manager, who was moving through the huge operation on the sound stage dressed in a floor-length wolf fur coat. But then, I was quite aware that managers and agents have often been known to be twice as flamboyant as the stars they look after.

At that first day of rehearsal, with the full benefit for the first time of the vast scale of the sound equipment and illuminated by the enormous lighting rig and towers, I heard all the *Queen* music I had never heard before. I suppose because I'd heard all the hits, all the obvious music, I thought I knew their work. I found that I was almost entirely ignorant of the substance of their career's six album output. Only a rehearsal maybe, but it was, of course, performed that day at the usual show-time level of decibels. I remember feeling physically overwhelmed by the sheer volume of sound.

I was also entirely impressed with the organisation of the whole operation which I found remarkable. The coordination of all the disparate but necessary elements involved in the staging of a rock 'n' roll tour is truly on a level akin to mounting a coronation and Gerry Stickles, *Queen*'s tour manager, has always been superb at his job. Through tight procedures, evident from that first day I joined the tour, he makes money for the band by saving them money. Every cent, every nickel, each penny is meticulously accounted for. Of course, I had been out on tour with the Royal Opera House Company and the Royal Ballet but ... the difference? Oh, easy. It's a hell of a lot more difficult getting the four members of a rock band onto the stage than any company of classical performers. Those four egos on the day of a performance are collectively and individually more unmanageable than an entire company in the classical arts.

So much rides on their individual shoulders. Each of the band members knows what is required of them and knows what would happen if one of them gets it wrong or if any part of the show fails them technically or in regard to timing. As Freddie always said, "You're only as good as your last show, dear." It's a fearsomely sharp goad which therefore prods them on to do ever better. Practically impossible. The pressure to do well for each of the two hundred thousand people crammed in to a stadium concert is explosive and when that pressure blows when someone on the team or in the crew gets it wrong, it's understandable. I felt that the band had every right to be pissed-off if something that went right on one show goes woefully wrong at the next. But although there were quite a few such explosions of temperament, there were very few sackings or instant dismissals in the time I was touring with *Queen*.

Right from the start, I was closer to Freddie than to the others. The first show was in Brighton and Freddie sent a car to collect me - a 'stretch' Mercedes limo wouldn't you know - from where I was living in a council flat on an estate in Lisson Grove to take me first to meet him at the now sadly disappeared Meridiana restaurant in the Fulham Road, where he was having lunch with Peter Straker and Paul Prenter and then to Brighton. The car was to also ferry us back because Brighton, being so close to London, was not an overnight venue.

I remember that first concert so vividly. It was the first time I had seen the persona as opposed to the person, the first time I had seen the persona of Freddie Mercury emerge on a stage in front of an audience and perform ... Really perform, reacting to the presence of that cheering crowd as their very welcome caused his constitutions's adrenaline to pump energy and power into the last little vein and sinew of his body. My reaction at seeing him perform was quite simple. It was one of awe. I had goose-bumps, I was excited ... I'd obviously felt all those physical symptoms of enjoyment when watching a great deal of opera. Ballet, even - Kenneth MacMillan's work is often physically exciting. But Freddie exuded that raw power which grabs you and shakes you. I will never get over that feeling of seeing someone who you live with every day, who you eat with and drink tea with and gossip about the newspapers over breakfast, stepping out onto a stage with the ability to hold the attention of a quarter of a million people in the palm of his hand. That power is truly mesmerising. He was often so tired that it seemed to us before he went on-stage sometimes that he would never get through the show. But then ... The symbiosis between his appearance on a stage and the audience's reception always produced a sort of chemical reaction in him which endowed him with the energy to not only get through the show but to triumph. A star, I suppose.

The process by which the man became the star was fascinating. When Freddie stepped out of the front gate of his home, he was at work. When he was on stage or in the studio, he was at the office. The persona emerged, came alive as he moved from private to public. They were different characters, the creator and the performer. The man who wrote the songs was a very different Freddie Mercury to the star who performed them. Mr. Mercury the messenger hadn't necessarily written the message.

But that six week *CRAZY* tour came to an end and everyone said goodbye. I was thanked, of course, but it was only ever casually suggested that they might call me in six months' time when Queen were next due to tour.

Ever pragmatic, I applied for a job as a telephone operator ... "Hello. Operator Service. Can I help you?" I stayed with British Telecom, as the company was known, for about three months until I had a second call from Paul Prenter inviting me to go out on tour with Queen again. This time, in North America.

Once again, I accepted immediately and hung up my headset.

America in those days was every European's wild frontier in a hundred different ways. Previously with the Royal Ballet I had been there twice on tour; the first one included Los Angeles, where I remember staying at the Holiday Inn opposite the Shrine Auditorium where the company were playing, Montreal, Vancouver, San Francisco (Oakland) and Mexico City. The second included Chicago, Washington and Houston.

America is so different to Britain which almost inculcates conservatism and inwardness in behaviour and outlook. America is so much bigger and - with no disrespect - brasher. Expansive. I think too that America also expects a great deal more, sort of ... 'Well, you're supposed to be so great, prove it!' America doesn't brook failure as much as Britain does.

At the beginning of their career, *Queen* were embraced by America although Freddie realised the need to never let up on performance standards for a moment. The U.S. music business was huge and even more competitive than Britain's. As far as the major touring cities were concerned, there was always a band in town, every night and the need to do well, to do best, in order to leave your impression on the buying mentality of the town the next day when the good burghers passed a record store was a pressure Freddie was very well aware of.

But as far as social life, offstage, was concerned, Freddie felt very much more relaxed in America. He didn't have that feeling that he was 'at work' as soon as he stepped out of the hotel door or his apartment lobby which he had in London although I have to emphasise that London was always, always home for him. His sense of anonymity - such a luxury for any celebrity - was perhaps increased by America's unfamiliar circumstances. In New York, for example, where he felt most relaxed, he used to walk around quite freely, never on his own but he didn't feel that constraint to always be in a car which kept him off the streets, as it were, in London. New Yorkers are used to seeing famous people walking about. It is, after all, a walking city.

To paraphrase a well-known nursery rhyme ...

When the tour was over, New York began to sing

Wasn't it a dainty dish to set before the King?

Or, in this case the King and *Queen* ... So, tempted, Freddie decided to spend longer in New York.

And I went on permanent salary, working solely for Freddie after 1982. In twelve years I never signed a contract and never had a job specification. But that I was on duty twenty fours hours a day, I was in no doubt. Holidays? When Freddie went on holiday, that was a holiday ... Your holiday too!

Freddie was also involved in Munich at the time as well as with his newly bought house in London, Garden Lodge, still being renovated and converted to his exacting standards; he spent as long periods in America as he did in Munich. When one's star waned, the other waxed. He always had that choice.

I was never in England for longer than six months a year because Freddie had opted for what is known as tax exile, Queen's schedule of touring and recording being set up around the world to ensure he could take greatest advantage of all the taxation legislation which governed his income. In London, I was still living in my own flat but in New York, my life with Freddie took on quite a different dimension.

In New York, the cost of the $1000-a-day hotel suites we stayed in for up to three months at a time finally gave way to his buying his own apartment on the forty third floor of the building at 425 East 58th Street with magnificent views north and south over the East River. You could see seven bridges from its balcony and I remember how excited Freddie was during the celebrations for the hundredth anniversary of the Brooklyn Bridge which we watched simultaneously both from the balcony and on the television.

The apartment had belonged to a senator or congressman by the name of Gray and it was bought from his widow. Gray by name and grey by colour. Most things were grey. Four bedrooms, five bathrooms, the den decorated in gray men's suiting fabric, a mirrored and closeted bedroom, dining room with silver coloured satin on the walls ... Ironically, bearing in mind the apartment's new owner was a man who so loved to decorate houses and refurbish and consult with designers and craftspeople, apartment 43E remained just as it had been bought. It was almost as though Freddie knew that having once bought it, he was to leave it only rarely to return.

The same thing happened in Munich with the apartment he shared with Barbara Valentin.

But for the years he spent in the thrall of this transatlantic life, he pursued both the work ethic and the pleasure principle with equal vigour. He was somewhat taken over by the constant clash of cultures and even began to let his beautifully enunciated English accent slip into some Americanisms which I felt didn't sit comfortably even on his admittedly broad cultural shoulders. What am I saying? They sounded *awful*!

Although Freddie was always open to finding his 'Dearest Him', (and found several temporary candidates along the way), no one emerged as contender for very long. Had they done so, Freddie would have been quite content to stay at home ... For a while. But that person would have had to have been someone very strong, tough enough in character to be able to fight back, to say 'No', mean it and stick to it; someone who understood, really understood Freddie's work and what he was about not only as a rock star but as a creator too.

In the absence of that person emerging, Freddie continued the search and I have to give him all credit for diligence for he really searched quite hard! Looks were then never an important factor in his choice of partners and, to be fair, his expectations of character too were not high. He was quite aware that most people who latched onto him were doing so *also* - not necessarily only - but *also* because he was who he was. He was always prepared to be let down in personal and social relationships and, in fact, expected to be. It made the wonderfully pleasant surprises of being *not* let down exquisitely delicious and there were indeed people who surprised him. Amongst them, his friend Thor, who now lives and nurses in San Diego, met Freddie in New York and under his own steam - with no tickets bought and paid for - turned up at the *Queen* gig a couple of days later miles away in Philadelphia. Freddie was bowled over. They remained friends until Freddie died.

It was perhaps no coincidence that the love affair with America was somewhat compromised by the reception that *Break Free* had. I fancy that the Bible Belt didn't like seeing a rock star in a bra. Homophobic tendencies were aroused and a lot of the punters' love affair both with

Freddie and *Queen* were proportionately compromised. Breaking free was done on Harley Davidsons or in souped-up Corvettes, not in drag! Real men and all that ... Americans don't have that indulgence for straight men dressing up as women, however much a pantomime parody the video of the song was. The cooling off was definitely punter-led. The industry, after all, will accept anything as long it yields income. Look at ... Oh, never mind.

So, as the title of the Tom Wolfe novel proclaims: Look Homeward Angel ... London calling, London calling ...

By the beginning of 1985, several factors conspired, one being that Joe Fanelli had come back to work for Freddie, having worked as a chef in several London restaurants, notably in Pimlico. Joe was based as much in Munich as anywhere although he obviously accompanied Freddie where required. The second factor was that Freddie had met Jim and that relationship was beginning to assume a significance over others. The final factor was that after so many years, Garden Lodge was at long last ready to be re-occupied.

Initially, rather surprisingly, Freddie seemed most reluctant to move in. In fact I was the first one to move into Garden Lodge and lived there for about eight months on my own. When Freddie was in London he stayed at Stafford Terrace which had been his home for so long and where he obviously felt safe and secure. It was indeed at Stafford Terrace that I re-met Jim Hutton for the first time. I really was quite amazed both that he remembered me from long ago Selfridges days and also about how small was the world we all lived in! Joe, truly independent as always, shuttled back and forth from Munich whilst Freddie took his time to make up his mind ...

One Friday, much later in 1985, Freddie finally decided that he would see, just *see* what a weekend was like at Garden Lodge. Significantly he did not bring his cats Oscar and Tiffany with him. He must have enjoyed his new home because on Monday, the cats were summoned and were also duly installed in their new home.

And so the scene was set for the rest of The Real Life.

Two things stand out like beacons for me when I look back over being 'caught in the landslide' as I believe this section is called, Freddie's creativity and the events leading up to and surrounding *Barcelona*.

I honestly don't think that Freddie had any overview whatsoever of his career. He had no master plan at all. He was far too pragmatic and he wouldn't have had the patience for long-term planning and strategies. His life and work was a progression, a natural development, one thing leading from another, yesterday's achievements being the tools he used to create tomorrow's. All the solo work that was undertaken was the artistic expression which they all knew could never be achieved within *Queen*. His desire to use strings, for example, was a facility in which Freddie knew he could never indulge within his *Queen* work. To have the freedom both to create, then to experiment and finally to make real was an essential outlet for Freddie; hence *Mr. Bad Guy*. Sometimes he had to be Mr. Bad Guy. It was either that or be consumed from within.

Objectively, he never expected his music to live forever. As far as he was concerned, his music was his job and as long as people continued to derive pleasure from his work he would keep working. Watching and being with him while he wrote was, for me, a really memorable experience. Although there were no outward signs that he would be in a writing mood - no broodiness or pacing up and down or anything - he would never allow me to forget to carry paper and pencil wherever we went, just in case ... It might only be a phrase or a couple of lines of lyrics that he'd tell me to scribble down but his moments would come anywhere. In the middle of a show, in a restaurant ... Most often on an aeroplane which is where "... (—) stains on my pillow ..." was rendered immortal!

I can't say - because it was always chicken and egg - whether he wrote lyrics or music first but music he always heard in his head and *usually* I believe the melodies or snatches of music preceded the lyrics. He'd hum something and then rush to get to the piano. When he did, he'd shout for me and I'd sit next to him and write down the chord names which he'd call out to me - "G" or "E Flat" or whatever. I suppose I was his amanuensis. Later, the notes I'd written down and the accompanying chords would revive the necessary memory of the more complete tune and he'd be able to recreate it, often using that strange musical writing he had.

If he had a favourite song, by the way, I think it was *Somebody to Love*.

If I was a help in any other way, I think it must have been by introducing Freddie to my own passion, opera. Which in turn brings me on to the whole subject of *Barcelona*.

From the very earliest times we were together, Freddie had always banged on about opera and although he'd obviously heard a lot of my records playing, it had never been a concentrated thing. So, in 1983, I finally took the situation in hand and bought us all tickets to go to Covent Garden to see Verdi's *Un Ballo In Maschera* at The Royal Opera House.

There was a fourth person with as I seem to remember and Joe, the third in the party, admittedly fell asleep. However, Freddie was enrapt by Pavarotti's performance in the first act.

By the beginning of the second, when Montserrat Caballé came on to sing her few phrases in the trio at the beginning of that act, Freddie was hooked and was instantly caught by her voice. "Who is she?" "What's going on, what's happening now?" It was instant admiration and thereafter, spurred on by my playing him many of her recordings, Freddie fell in love with Montserrat's voice.

It has to be said that it was with voices he became involved, not with the art form as a whole. I don't think he had the patience for it. He had a very low boredom threshold and, perhaps born from all those hours of sitting at the recording desk in the studio, Freddie seemed to have what I can only describe as a fast-forward-and-rewind mentality to a lot of the performing arts. I took him to see Georges Bizet's *Carmen* with Jose Carerras and Agnes Baltsa for example and he didn't take to it at all. Yet, alternatively, he could watch a film of *Carmen* precisely because he knew he could get up and do something else in the bits that bored him.

Though the story of his announcing in the Spanish media his admiration for her is absolutely true and though she was indubitably intrigued by the idea of working with him, Freddie's ultimate involvement with Montserrat Caballé was also a great deal to do with business.

As a background, for some time, Jim Beach had been talking to Carlos, Montserrat's brother and business manager. Once the idea had been mooted, the possibility of Freddie and Montserrat performing as a duet a potential theme for the 1992 Olympic Games in her home city of Barcelona was a huge lever to ease the creative rolling stone down the slope. To have such a huge worldwide television audience was too great a temptation for anyone, including Freddie, to ignore. He took audience statistics very seriously.

When they were finally set to meet, Freddie found he was holding a double-edged sword. On one hand he couldn't quite believe that he could be working with the voice he so adored and on the other couldn't believe he *would* be working with Montserrat Caballé, the person. He, I, Jim Beach and Mike Moran set off for Barcelona with a very roughly recorded cassette tape of four of their songs on which Freddie had had to pretend to sing the part he had in mind for Montserrat. Needless to say, not only did she like the songs but she loved the notion that Freddie had pretended to sing as her. When it had been explained to her what the word 'album' meant - "Album? What eez thees album?" - she embraced the project wholeheartedly, announcing that there was little point in just doing one of the songs!

I think that *Barcelona* was the first time he really pleased himself. Even if the finished album had never been released, he wouldn't have complained. After the first take in the studio of Montserrat's part on *Barcelona* Freddie just grinned and grinned with glee - "I've finally got her voice!" - for as you know, like with Straker, for example, Freddie was capable of being very envious of other people's talents. Never jealous, mind ... I think it's good to be envious. Provides a great spur.

The Sunday after that Tuesday meeting in Barcelona, Montserrat was due to sing at the Royal Opera House in Covent Garden. After her two and a half hour show, she and her niece Montse came round to Garden Lodge. It was a night I shall never, ever forget. After a glass of champagne which then flowed all night, it didn't take them long to gravitate to the piano. Mostly Mike Moran played and as he extemporised, anticipating the directions Freddie and Montserrat's voices were taking, the singers sang. They composed as they sang, nothing specific but just exploring, with Mike, vocal ideas which they took up, tossed back and forward, played with and, if they all approved of the end result, kept and incorporated. It was magic. Montse and I watched in absolute amazement, I especially feeling very, very proud.

Freddie was amazed at the amount that Montserrat smoked and told her off, saying that he was terrified what Carlos would do to him if he found out that they had stayed up all night smoking and drinking! They were very natural with each other that night, completely at ease and totally relaxed, un-encumbered by either her pressures of work and schedule and his pressures born of being writer, arranger, producer and performer. When they worked in the studio, there was never the fluidity and oneness that they achieved that first night when they 'jammed' together.

But there was so much more left ... So much more they would have each liked to have done together. Instead, Montsy had to sing alone and for him she attended the first performance of European Chamber Opera's production of Verdi's *Il Trovatore* at The Banqueting Hall in Westminster after he'd gone.

But there was a ways to go yet.

From 1987, it doesn't need to be pointed out again really but Freddie stopped doing anything publicly and The Real life took yet another turn.

I never thought that I would be following my mother in her nursing footsteps but that's what I had to learn to do. We *had* to. And all of course with the shadow of *The Secret* hanging over us all the time. Every day, waking up knowing that you could tell no one, could talk about it to no one. Freddie kept huge areas of his illness to himself. And fair enough. He was the acute sufferer at that point and it's up to the person concerned to whom or when he confides his business.

He actually began to keep some people away. He really didn't want anyone who wasn't very close to him to see him going downhill. There was a point when he began to reassemble the pieces of his life, making sure that he only saw the faces he wanted to see, people who didn't cause him any distress. These people he told of his illness. Though I'm sure they knew, he didn't actually tell the band until a little less than a year before he died. Telling someone, imparting that sort of confidence requires a quantum leap of both resolve and perspective. Dying turns every other perspective on its head. We live expecting to live, not to die.

Freddie sort of re-formed his life, reconstituted what he needed for his short future from his long, rich past, often like an archaeologist. Dave Clark was wonderful to him as was Tony King. Elton John too, of course. Especially Elton for he took it all very personally and deeply.

The team from the Westminster Hospital were wonderful. From the oncologist who tried to relieve the Kaposi's Sarcoma to the skin specialist ... Wonderful. They were of course just as bound by *The Secret* as we all were and Freddie was in many ways the model patient. People never bothered him as anything but a patient or let their private perceptions of treating a big star get in the way of their work and, therefore, his comfort. About a year later, I used to take a friend into the Westminster and the same team treated my un-famous friend in absolutely the same way that Freddie was treated, the only difference being that Freddie was seen at seven in the morning whilst my friend was able to be seen at a more normal hour in the day's appointments.

It's amazing how quickly you learn to be able to do things you never expected you'd have to do. The human being is truly an adaptable machine. Joe and I nursed Freddie in the main, administering his medicines to him via the Hickman line inserted into his upper chest. It worked very well. But drugs are poisons and there came a time when it was very, very obvious that their effect would never again be remedial.

Freddie was never alone. For the last weeks of his life there was someone with him all day and all night. We would take it in turns, Jim, Joe and I to be with him and stay awake all night and then take shifts during the days. I have to say that he was in complete control of his life right until the end and I also have to say that when the quality of his life started to deteriorate beyond being bearable, he would, if he'd been able, rather have taken himself off to the vet and asked for an injection. He would have seen such an action as not only expedient but kind. It was, after all, exactly what he would have offered to his adored cats.

If I'm not back again this time tomorrow
Carry on, carry on...

PART III

FINAL THOUGHTS

In writing and assembling this book, we have of course learned a lot more about Freddie than we knew and this we were expecting. We have also learned a lot more about his friends and colleagues, much of which we did not know and some aspects of which we were not expecting.

The more people talked to us about their friend, the more we realised that at least we were talking about the same man. So many times in talking to people with whom a friend is sheared, the friend in question has been a different man to different people. Freddie was one man. This is not to say he was in any way a simple character.

Freddie Mercury was an elaborately and carefully constructed concept which could only have life breathed into it because it was built by a man who had been well-taught and who was himself a shrewd and discriminating observer of the mistakes that others made. He knew his strength and he equally knew his weaknesses and that qualification alone is one which can be used by everyone and which is reason enough for him to be properly understood.

We started writing this book because we wanted our friend to have as many memorials as possible. Since we started to write, there has been a massive concert at Wembley and we believe, another one planned by performers who were not able to participate in the Wembley show. Peter Freestone has marvellously organised a classical recital with Freddie's close friend Montserrat Caballé. There have been several picture books, a sort of biography and now... this.

It's the only memorial that we and the friends who have herein contributed can raise to him. There are many people who were unable to say anything at the time of his illness and death because Freddie didn't want to burden them with the knowledge of his condition.

Now he has died, there is no grave, there is no place where we can go knowing that his ashes are there; there will not be a plot in Poet's Corner or a grand memorial service in Westminster Abbey or even St. Martin's or even the Actors' Church in Covent Garden. There is no kitchen table we can gather round to be sad and swap stories and reminisce about the days of our lives. There are videos, several books and of course lots and lots of recordings.

Even dabbling on the edges of the rock business once again, we have been reminded of the huge power which is generated by the shibboleth of success and wealth and it is sobering to realise that this power was generated by just one man.

Alternatively, we have been amazed by how many friends Freddie had; real friends. We have been amazed at their loyalty, their closeness and their integrity. In the course of collecting these tributes, we were often shocked by the depth of grief that his death plumbed, grief that in many cases is still emerging and which perhaps will never be put to rest.

It would not surprise us if we published a request for the readers of this book to send in their own tributes to Freddie and their thanks for all the good times in their own lives which they will forever associate with him and his music, we could fill a hundred such volumes as this with ease. It also goes without saying that there are many of his friends who we would have like to approach but who, through constraints of time and geography we were unable to ask. To these people, we apologise and trust they will understand.

However, for the time being, to all those contributors who have given their time, attention and consideration to what is printed within these pages, thank you.

Freddie died on November 24th 1991. He was superbly cared for on a daily and most intimate basis by Joe Fanelli, Peter Freestone, Gerry Giddings and of course Jim Hutton. All of these acted as nurses as well as confidantes and carers to a degree way beyond both love and any call of duty. Freddie was indeed fortunate to have such an indefatigable support system, which together with Mary and her son Richard helped him through his final days. Freddie was also much helped by Dave Clark's friendship and he was utterly thrilled when Elton John came to visit him. Even at that late stage, Freddie still demanded vindication and Elton's visits and his wonderful birthday gift did much raise his spirits.

David Evans
David Minns

DERRICK BRANCHE

We obviously met up after we'd been in England for some time, but I lost touch with Freddie after 1976. I went on treading the boards and he went on cranking out his latest version of that boogie woogie piano.

He also added lead singer to the repertoire I'd recognised from school days. It was a position I never thought he would adopt. I think the reticence that not only I but others noticed was resolved somewhat after he came to term with his sexuality. As I mentioned earlier, St. Peter, Panchgani, was no different to all the other public schools of the boarding variety throughout the world and pupils there, including Freddie, went through their own fair share of confusion and incomprehension as puberty overtook them and their bodies began giving their minds conflicting signals. As we know, most people - either boys or girls - work their way through that single sex situation and emerge on the other side clear as to their orientation. I think it took Freddie a lot longer than most to come to terms with the way life had cast him. As soon as he did, I believe it allowed him to be able to control the other areas of his confusion and to marshal his obviously boundless talents to become the person we are now remembering.

I'm glad he was able to for it enabled him to really enjoy the tragically foreshortened life he led.

It broke my heart that night he died.

Watching the tribute concert from Wembley really devastated me. Only a short time before, I'd lost two other friends, first Bob Mosher and then Victor Espinoza. Watching all those people crammed into the stadium paying tribute to Freddie just cracked me up. I cried and after I'd cried I felt drained, empty, like there was nothing left.

My own life suddenly seemed so short; it seemed that we had no sooner left school that he was dead. When someone who has been that close to you dies, someone who'd always been there, something of you dies too, for there's no longer anyone to remember with, no one left to recall those wonderful days when we were the best rock band in Panchgani and girls came to scream at us when we played, so young and innocent and so full of hopes and dreams.

I'm left with very lonely memories.

I miss the child that Freddie always was. That child has gone, once and for all, and all the joy and laughter that he'd given me whilst we were at school and which he continued to give to the rest of the world has also gone forever.

DAVID MINNS

In more recent years, life had become calmer for both Freddie and myself. Time had done it's work as the great healer. However, one is naturally thrown back into occasional reassessment of the past and the result is that you end up coming to terms with it by usually either hating the person whom you've left and everyone around them or ignoring them or still carrying a torch for them.

In my case, it was none of these things. I couldn't hate him, for who could hate someone like Freddie, yet neither did I kid myself into even imagining that we would ever be best friends again. Our close friendship was a closed chapter. Eventually, I had taught myself to withdraw although it was very difficult when the person from whom you are retreating was constantly on the radio and television and whose existence permeated every corner of the world in which I still was making my living. It was this continuing reminder of his presence which could still make me angry although my anger was directed not at Freddie but at what fame does.

Of course, in the end I had to thank him for it all, because the experience made me tougher on the inside and taught me how to cope for myself and for others. I really believe that losing a friend can be like a divorce which in turn is a bereavement of sorts. I think I grieved more for the loss of him then than I have had to now.

In the last year of his life, though I didn't see him, I constantly thought of him, prayed for him and thankfully was kept informed of his health by our other friends. I respect his wish not to expose himself to too many people. I had nursed my friend Janet O'Hanlon, the film publicity consultant, through her illness. I had also lost my brother in the same week as Janet died and subsequently a nephew, from cancer, in 1990. I had, therefore, the utmost respect for Freddie who was obviously making such a valiant effort to retain as much dignity as possible whilst making his exit.

This exit was systematically, it seems, frustrated by certain sections of the press. Latterly, this was exacerbated by revelations made by an ex-employee of Freddie, Paul Prenter. Thankfully, in many people's books, or should I say, codes of ethics, we do not write about our friends in the tabloids for gain or revenge. It is an unwritten rule that if you work or are close friends with someone in the public eye, you are in a privileged position and breaking those rules is unforgivable. Freddie never used the press to vent his anger or personal feelings about anyone. In fact, though he was constantly in the press and was the tabloids' dream victim for their periodic character assassinations, he did not court or curry their attention. Others around him may have perpetrated myths which the press then took only to blow up to legendary proportions. There are of course the exceptions amongst journalists. They know who they are: David Wigg, Nina Myskow, Paul Gambaccini amongst them but then they knew Freddie as a friend.

I am not going to remember Freddie as the sad victim of a dread disease but for the often hysterical and crazy times we all shared. He was one of the funniest people you could ever wish to have met. In the early days, I recall the banter between Freddie and Elton John who seemed to bring out the worst, yet the best of each other's sense of humour. It was the general practice that whilst both superstars were touring, pseudonyms were used around the world at all hotel's stopovers for the purpose of room reservations. This prevented unwanted telephone calls and deterred fans from turning up uninvited.

During a weekend we all spent at Elton's house in Old Windsor, we fell prey to Elton's habit of handing out pseudonyms which on this occasion he delivered by means of his impersonation of dame Edith Evans playing Lady

Bracknell. He ceremoniously announced:

"I've got yours, Freddie, already... Melina! Melina Mercury - geddit!!" (Melina Mercouri - goddit?).

I didn't know whether to laugh or cry. Freddie was speechless - for once. Subsequently, he fell in with the game and the rest of the weekend was spent naming people. I got to be Dilys, presumably after Dilys Powell; Rod Stewart got to be Phyllis, after Phyllis Diller. Everyone's favourite remained Elton's, bestowed by Tony King; in my mind, Elton will forever be Sharon Cavendish.

It was all good clean fun, meant with all the best intentions. To see Freddie laughing uproariously, rocking backwards and forwards yet at the same time trying to cover his mouth with his hand to disguise his teeth, which he admitted were sadly not his best feature, is an image that will haunt me for the rest of my life.

Even after all these years, I could not bring myself to watch or listen to the tribute concert broadcast from Wembley Stadium this year. It was a glorious early summer evening and I decided to have a barbecue with friends in the garden. It had been our intention to listen to the concert on the radio. A song came on which held particularly vivid memories. It destroyed me emotionally. I think the other members of *Queen* were really brave to attempt such a difficult concert. It must have been hell without Freddie.

DAVID EVANS

I felt more deeply for Freddie with Aids than I had felt for any other of my friends. I don't know why this should have been so but it was so. Maybe the impression of his life was more deeply branded into my psyche; maybe when you have famous friends, however much you think their fame doesn't affect you, it does, after all; after all you have so self-congratulatingly thought about yourself, how strong you've been in not being drawn in, how you weren't fooled by it, taken in by it. I can hear him saying it:

"Well dear, you were. So what?"

So what indeed. Except that I now dream about him. It's got to be that bad. But at least I dream about him whole, not ravaged and hurt and wounded like some shrunken, starved and long-legged wading bird who'd shuffle up to you for a kiss and look at you with eyes that would have drowned you in their infinite knowledge and wisdom. That's what he was like, towards the end and his state of perceived grace convinced me that there has to be some magical, alchemical process that those who are about to die undergo for I perceive them only as being charged with a huge and limitless knowledge which I do not possess and at which I can only marvel. So, I'm wrong. So what? Let me believe it because I find it comforting and, in the absence of any just reason for this current carnage, it is a convenient explanation. As far as I am concerned, without such personal rationales, we would all, surely, be mad by now?

I'm glad he went like he did. I'm glad he didn't have to make another dash for his car, hobbling as fast as he could safely carry himself to avoid another encounter with the newspapers. I'm glad they were robbed of being able to point the ink-stained finger and say: "Told you so... Knew you had it all the time. Now, how do you *feel*?"

I restrained my anger concerning those fine ladies and gentlemen of the fabulous column inch 'til one day I could stand it no more. When one newspaper carried a front page story, taken as Freddie returned to his car from a shop he'd been patronising. I rang the paper and complained and also wrote to the Press Council. To do that sorry body what little justice it may be due, my letter was forwarded to the newspaper concerned. The reply, in precis, explained basically that as Freddie had consciously sought and nurtured publicity in order to rise to fame, it was only fair that the same publicity be used to explore that fame and report it faithfully to his fans who after all were directly and only persuaded by his publicity machinations to ascribe fame to him! The newspaper obviously was trying to make itself believe that it performed a public service. It's a specious argument but scratch that plausible surface and you find the same people who, reincarnated a century ago, both exhibited and paid to see The Elephant Man. Such behaviour is not civilised and cannot be justified by civilised people although I do rather believe that Rupert Everett wrote in Hello,

Darling, Are You Working?: "You get what you want in the form you deserve..." But, if we have the press we deserve can it really be that we have made so little progress as a society since we watched disembowelments at Tyburn, the cavorting of the insane at Bedlam and the pain of The Elephant Man at Victorian pleasure grounds? If I believed we *had* made such progress, would I then have to believe that only 'nice' people buy *Queen* records and only 'nice' people made Freddie a star? If that were true, no one would buy any newspapers which sells copies because of their victims' shame, humiliation and embarrassment, and where no real public interest is finally served.

I rang Joe Fanelli at Freddie's house to see if I should take my case any further and he advised me to retreat. I did, reluctantly.

During his final year, I watched as Freddie bravely clung to every hand-held he could find to keep him upright and moving. Together, with Joe Fanelli, Freddie's cook and confidante, we concocted an outrageous cook book... 'Entertaining Mister Mercury' it was going to be called and Fred was going to see to all the artwork and photography and use all his wonderful pieces of glass, china and brocantage to illustrate Joe's fine food. He organised the redecoration and furnishing of a flat he used whilst staying in Montreux where he frequently spent time; he devoured saleroom catalogues from the major auction houses and began to buy voraciously, setting what I believe is the saleroom record for the price paid for a piece of Lalique glass. He became more deeply interested in painting than hitherto and continued to add to is Meissen collection. For the most part, he never allowed us to believe that his plans and schemes were merely buttresses propping up an imminently terminal case of collapse.

I'm glad he spent and enjoyed spending his money. He'd earned it and compared to some I know, although he had been generous, he had never thrown his money away. He was always careful. Over lunch one day in the beautiful conservatory which had been built against the mews wall in his garden, he told me he was worried about money, about how much things were costing. Nothing was specified but his outgoings were never far from his mind.

He last came over to lunch with Tony King. We had a lovely day, he, Tony, Nigel and I, just giggling and gossiping which he loved to do. Sadly, he was too weak to climb the stairs to view the alterations which had been created, the bedroom, bathroom and dressing room suite which he had urged and advised us to construct on the lines of his own at Logan Place. Gone was talk of high-flying things, of recent triumphs and looming challenges. Instead, I remember us talking endlessly about the dangers of leaky showers and how he'd just about given up on his own... He announced to Tony King that Nigel and I were the only ones of his friends who ever asked him out. I'm sure, in fact I know, that this is absolutely not true but it seemed an infinitely sad thing fir him to have said and I mention it only to try and convey how occasionally he must have felt when confronted with returning to his own house where, however much he felt safe and secure, he knew he had a lot of time to think.

A few days after that lunch I took some doughnuts over to Logan Place and called in for coffee and brunch. We sat round the kitchen table. I wondered how he managed the journey to Switzerland.

"It's not so bad now," he admitted. Since I stopped waiting in queues at immigration. F... it, I thought one day, Liz Taylor wouldn't put up with this, why should I?"

He must have made his traditional little bit of fuss and thereafter was apparently whisked off on his own in another chauffeur driven car across the Tarmac.

"Good for you," I said.

"Umm," he said, a doubt having crossed his mind. He laughed. "Mind you, dear," he giggled, "last time, I was sitting in that car thinking... I don't know this man. Just *who* is driving this car? Perhaps it's all a front? Perhaps... yeek! Am I being kidnapped?"

Terry Giddings, Freddie's driver and great friend, drove Peter, Freddie and I to Christie's auction rooms in King Street where we viewed an up-coming sale of paintings. I remember Freddie's choices for which Peter was to bid later at the sale. They were choices in which I concurred wholeheartedly, outstanding, amongst which was a lovely Victorian oil of a laughing, carefree Mediterranean girl, a painting so full of life it fairly glowed off the wall. We wandered round, viewing the other pictures. People were looking at him. So what, I thought. The words of Bohemian Rhapsody echoed in my ears: 'Nothing really matters, anyone can see, nothing really matters... to me'.

We kissed and embraced on the pavement outside and the Mercedes pulled away from the kerb. He didn't usually turn and wave but this time, he did... It was the last time I saw him.

My book came out in November, dedicated, amongst others, to Freddie for without some of his experience I could never have written it. Somehow, life didn't take me across London to Logan Place. I was too busy... there was so much going on...

Liar.

I didn't see him again because, oddly, I didn't want to intrude. I felt that death was a very private thing and that, he should be left alone to do it his way. He wasn't alone. He was surrounded by those who cared for him deeply and on a daily basis and by those who loved him.

The night before his funeral I was in Huddersfield being interviewed about my book. I was going to stay the night. I'm glad I didn't for Peter Freestone 'phoned from Logan Place and left a message with Nigel that I would be welcome at the funeral.

The day dawned dull and damp and I drove out to the West London Crematorium to what was supposed to be a quiet, private, family funeral.

"Strange," Peter had said to Nigel when he'd called, "it's as though he's not ours any more. The family have taken him back."

They and the world soon reclaimed him for Logan Place and Freddie's garden was crammed with flowers from the good and the great as well as the merely mourning.

I knew the funeral wasn't going to be private. Four policemen were standing at the gate of the crematorium. I drove up and lowered my window:

"Mr. Bulsara's funeral," I said, weakly, using the name Freddie had given up so many years before and to which he was now being returned, in death, by those who had given him birth. For a moment, the policeman looked puzzled and then light seeped in.

"Ah," he said, almost with a sad wisdom. "Drive through, sir."

As soon as I parked the car, I realised I was not alone. The world's media were gathered at a none too respectful distance but one which had clearly been agreed with someone. Far enough away not to be intrusive... As I waited to enter the crematorium chapel, I overheard one hack say to another in glottal tone:

"D'jer getanyfink?"

"Lovely one wiv Elton puttin' 'is arm round Brian May..." came the reply.

After the service, intoned by two parsee priests using harmonies and chants which Freddie himself must have used as a basis of inspiration for so much of his layering studio techniques, we emerged from the chapel to be photographed in turn by Richard Young. I could have laughed except I was crying. I'm not used to being photographed whilst in the throes of sobbing publicity. For those of you who aren't familiar with café society, Richard Young is the paparazzi's paparazzo. I found it strange that he should be there at all in a working capacity.

Perhaps I was wrong in assuming that Freddie hadn't courted publicity but, in those circumstances especially, I don't think so.

I was pursued back to my car by three reporters whom I could have cheerfully cursed but restrained myself. They almost ran after me, notebooks poised, firing questions about the form of service, the events inside the chapel, who, what, where, how and why?

I drove home in tears, changed my clothed and did some gardening. I have an azalea which Freddie gave me on the day he confided the state of his health to me. I had transplanted it after it had finished flowering and it was growing strongly and vigorously at the corner of the lawn. I weeded around it and willed it to survive the coming winter. It was, after all, a delicate indoor specimen, forced to bloom perhaps to soon and therefore open to nature's risks.

I hope, if there is an after-life, Freddie's not too upset at my doing this book. He was always so private, yet so public. I will never, never forget him and have already added his face to those ageless and tireless friends who have gone on before me, friends who will never grow older as we who are left behind shall, condemned indubitably to age and wither. We are now in the only recently vacated waiting room, expecting the return of the same chariot, one day, wondering all the while but hopefully not quite as afraid as before. For, if they have climbed aboard, so can we...

EDDIE HOWELL

Musically, I'm not sure how many people know this, but Freddie sang sharp. He didn't know it, but he did. Whether he had perfect pitch or not I don't know but to pit his voice against an instrument in constant pitch, his voice would always be very slightly sharp. Most people sing flat; I sing flat and sharp singing is scientifically more pleasing to the human ear than even perfectly pitched singing for the voice dances just above the note implying a freedom of spirit which is not tied to this earth. Lots of great singers, like Caruso, sang sharp; Sinatra certainly does. I mention this only because as a final thought about him, whenever I hear Freddie's voice that's what springs to my mind.

As to the man, I felt that he wanted to love everyone. I'm sure that this diminished as his relationship with people wore on but I was conscious of the fact that he very much wanted to be fond of people. With me as with most people, he was never particularly demonstrative although you were very aware that he wanted you to like him back; he desperately wanted you to like him. I found that very endearing as I felt a little in awe of the situation I found myself in as Freddie was the hottest shot around at the time of the recording.

There was always an air of mystery surrounding Freddie. Undercurrents of surmise and assessment were always swirling in the atmosphere surrounding him. He realised that people thought him an enigma and I felt that more than anything he wanted to be a man of the people as well as living up to his public persona. It was almost as though he knew that he couldn't be either, that in some way he was fated not to be. I feel it was his resulting frustration which was so tangible and which caused the presence of that perpetual question mark he sported instead of the halo.

PETER STRAKER

I'm writing this a year later. There's a sadness that I wasn't around for the last year of his life. I was working very hard in Ken Hill's *Phantom of the Opera*, touring, away from London. It was also, for some reason that I still don't completely understand, Freddie's wish not to see me. Theories and suppositions have been put forward by many others. I think I understand, within my mind's eye, but in the long run whatever makes someone who is suffering happy, we who are alive and who have survived can only accept.

Strangely, Freddie Mercury sort of still lives. His music is just everywhere. I've just been in Japan with the aforesaid Phantom and because I knew Freddie loved Japan so much, I was very much aware of his continuing presence. Returning to England, I found that *Barcelona* is in the charts again and so although I don't see him, I still hear him and I miss him.

NINA MYSKOW

I feel privileged to have known him. It sounds such a cliché but in the event it is all one can say. Without him, I would have never gone to South America. That's just for starters.

More importantly, I would certainly never have had an insight into the complexities of a character who was a complete dichotomy. The difference between the on-stage Freddie, in complete command and control over so many people, a kind of benevolent dictator... the difference between that complete extrovert and the private Freddie. Because this difference was so extreme, having known him makes it easier to understand things about myself and about other people. He allowed himself to be painted so either black or white... The grey areas he kept very much to himself. He was an amazing example of all sorts of human emotions. He was a screen upon which you could project all your own doubts and insecurities.

In the beginning, I had another reason to be fascinated with Freddie. My interest in him had an extra, very personal dimension for when I first got to know Freddie, I was still very much in love with a man who was gay. I could not help but empathise strongly with Mary and, obviously, took a particular interest in her and Freddie's relationship if only to see if it could work out, if it would work out. I suppose that was rather selfish of me. Oddly enough, it wasn't something I ever discussed with Freddie. I suppose when I had access to him for that sort of conversation, I wasn't capable of analysing my own doomed relationship in which there was a lot of self-deception. Because I severed all connections in my own relationship in 1982 as the only way of being able to survive and have a life of my own, I have to admit to an admiration for Mary. She was the one who had to come to terms with Freddie's sexuality. She was the one who had to compromise. The fact that they salvaged an enduring friendship from the wreck of a love affair must be down to her tenacity. I also admire Freddie for recognising what she must have meant to him. I couldn't have done it.

The last time I saw Freddie was at a party at Groucho's after the Brits Awards in 1990. I was extremely drunk and, I fancy, pretty badly behaved. Freddie was sitting with his back against the wall at a table upstairs in a very crowded room. I think Roger was at the same table. I thought Freddie looked rather thin and drawn and he was rather quiet and shy. I think he was pleased to see me.. I wish I'd been more sober, I would have paid more attention. All I can remember is leaping to my feet to embrace Anita Dobson as she appeared through the crowd with Brian May, forgetting I had a full glass of champagne in my hand which went all over her frock as I expansively shouted: "Darling!" The rest is a blur.

I remember reading Fleet Street murmurings that Freddie was gravely ill and I didn't really check them out as I didn't want to contemplate any ghastly truth. I suppose deep inside, I knew the worst. At one point in the last year, I remember asking John Reid about Freddie and he confirmed my fears.

I suppose one always has regrets after someone dies. I've always said that in life you never regret what you do but only what you fail to do and it's like that with Freddie. I'd had his 'phone number at Logan Place since I'd gone to his fortieth birthday Mad Hatters' Sunday party but I never dared ring him. I never presumed. I don't mean to sound humble but one always imagines that there are far more important people, other closer friends and you never want to shove yourself forward or to pry. Although I'd given up Fleet street in 1987, I was still very aware that people thought of me as a journalist and therefore was very wary of putting myself in a position which might be miscon-strued. I'd hate anyone to think I was using them, abusing them.

I think I realised how close it must be to the end the Thursday before he died. I called David Evans to tell him we couldn't come to dinner the following night as arranged as I had to go to Birmingham for a TV show. David and I hadn't had a great deal of contact lately so there hadn't been any conversation about Freddie. When we'd rearranged dinner, I asked David how Freddie was and added that I knew he couldn't really say. I knew enough that Freddie wanted it that way. I wondered if it would be alright to send a card and David encouraged me, adding that I might not get a reply but at least Freddie would know.

On the Saturday night, the *News of the World* rang me at home. A features editor called Tony Harris who'd been on *The Sun* when I'd gone to South America remembered that I knew him. He told me that *Queen* had issued a statement confirming that Freddie had Aids. Tony Harris asked me to comment. I must have said something like I was very sad and that if I could have waved a magic wand to have put things right. I would have. What I did know was that it must have been fairly near the end or else such statement would not have been issued. I put the 'phone down and just burst into tears.

On Monday morning, driving Grant to work, we heard the seven o'clock news on *Capital*. Although it was news that we were expecting, it was absolutely devastating. I can remember driving back through the West End to Hampstead, hardly able to see. Because I knew I had to do something positive, I hurled myself into my aerobics class at nine-thirty. It seemed to help in a way.

Twenty minutes after I got home, the phone rang. A TV producer from *BBC* Manchester was calling from *People Today* programme which goes out live weekday mornings from eleven thirty. They had read in the *News of the World* that I knew Freddie and wondered if I'd be prepared to comment on air that day just down the 'phone line. I agreed, thinking at least tat it would give me a chance to pay tribute to him in the way I hadn't been able to do during his last illness.

Five minutes later, they rang back and said they'd worked out that if they could get a car to me in five minutes they could get me to their

153   *FINAL THOUGHTS*

Millbank Studios. I was horrified. I was dripping with sweat, my hair like rats tails. In a way it made me laugh, this vanity at a time like that but Freddie would have understood! I hurled myself together, worked miracles with a hair dryer, flung on bucketfuls of make-up in the back of the taxi and found myself sitting in front of a camera waiting for the link to Manchester.

After the twelve o'clock news, there was due to be a seven minute film of Russell Grant in New York. Manchester told me they'd come to me after that. They also had a 'phone link with Dave Clark whom, they told me, was very upset. Because of Russell's filmed report, the Freddie tribute would be only four minutes long top whack. Typically, halfway through Russell's report, the film broke down and the Manchester presenter hurriedly opened up the link and fired a question at me. I was perfectly all right with it until the link between London and Manchester broke down. They turned then to Dave Clark on the 'phone. His voice sounded absolutely awful. He was obviously terribly upset. I sat and watched his picture on the studio monitor and listened to him saying that he'd been with Freddie the night before, at the end. To my amazement and sheer horror, the presenter asked totally crassly: "What was it like?" Up until that point I hadn't though about it myself, it was somehow too physical, too real, too definite. Sitting alone in that little studio, I just burst into tears. Dave, poor soul, said he really couldn't answer and, I think, succumbed to his emotions.

The link from Manchester to London was suddenly restored and there I was, caught by the camera, crying on screen. I can't really remember but I think I said that I felt a bit of a fool for that but that if you missed someone, you really missed them. Trying to be cheerful, I added that at least those who knew him and loved him and all those fans around the world would always have his music to keep him alive. I suppose clichés are clichés because they are true.

When I got back home, I rang Miriam Stoppard, the show's main presenter to apologise, in case she thought I'd been in some way unprofessional by being so emotional. Miriam was lovely about it and said, on the contrary, that if Freddie was the sort of 'chap' who inspired that sort of emotion, then he deserved to have someone express it publicly. She told me that watching me, she had lost it herself and had to do the closing link to the programme blinking back her own tears.

What came out of that day, for me, is something else I have to thank Freddie for. 1991 was a dreadful year for television. I had hardly worked at all and was completely broke. That one appearance on the People Today programme sparked off a regular contract with them which still continues. So, that was Freddie doing me a good turn. I firmly believe in circles. Just as you should never take revenge on anyone, life will do that for you, you should do things for other people without expecting any reward. It comes back to you eventually in ways you least expected.

MIKE MORAN

He's absolutely irreplaceable. He was my friend and I think of him everyday.

JACKY GUNN

I think it's been easier in a way for me than it's been for people like Jim and the other fans. After all, we had to deal with it directly.

The day after he died, though we were told to just let the phones ring, I couldn't. People just couldn't believe it. They had to be talked to. I felt that it helped me, helping them. I just told myself that every time I felt sad and wanted to cry, I just had to think of him as that larger than life person who made us feel so good.

I never thought of him as he was in those last months. At least I knew about what was going to happen. Thousands didn't. I sort of became Auntie Jackie. I never thought of him as gone. Strangely, because as his image is always with us, he's not gone at all.

I'll always put store on what he said to me, that thing about style... Do it with style. That's what I shall keep with me all my life.

JIM JENKINS

Difficult. I've thought about him every day since that awful news. It was one of the blackest moment of my life.

I couldn't go to work that Monday. Jacky helped me. Friends who came round helped too and we were crying and laughing. He's left me with some great memories and some great friends. All those closest to me I've met through knowing Freddie and *Queen*. There's so much we have left to watch and listen to. Watch the *Slightly Mad* video and that uplifts you. That was Freddie at his best, to me.

As a fan, I was very honoured to go to the twentieth anniversary celebration. I went over and said thank you for the wonderful seventeen years he'd given me.

He'll always be with me, 'til the day I go and join him.

PAUL GAMBACCINI

Even though I have warm and vivid memories of Freddie personally, the moment I think of first when someone mention his name is *Live Aid*.

I was part of the *BBC* broadcast team and I was doing the interviews backstage with the other artists. When *Queen* came on that afternoon there was an atmosphere backstage where all the artists shared this sense that *Queen* were stealing the show. Any community of artists has a wavelength but that afternoon, the message didn't even have to be verbalised. People just looked at each other and said: "They're stealing the show!"

The following week, the *BBC* audience panel gave its report and over 50% said that *Queen* had been the outstanding act. It would, surely, have been impossible to achieve that kind of consensus with so many great artists on the bill that day. But the way that band rehearsed and the way that Freddie, against his doctor's wishes I understand, went out and performed was incredible. The way he played simultaneously to the cameras and to the crowd, to me is the ultimate sort of professionalism in that broadcast concert situation.

I was there; I felt the wave that swept through the people and I'll never forget it.

GORDON ATKINSON

This is very difficult for me as my mind is still filled with the thoughts of his dying. He never complained and his anguish was more for his friends and family than for himself.

His bedroom was filled with flowers and Delilah, his tortoiseshell cat, was always poking her face out from beneath the covers when anyone visited.

On the night he died, I was telephoned in my car five minutes after I'd left the house to say that he'd stopped breathing. When I returned, he was lying there with a look of ecstasy on his face. His parents arrived for prayers and wondered if his face had been made up; he looked to be in such ecstasy.

It had been a long fight for him. For nearly five years he had carried on without question and the end, when it came, was sudden and peaceful.

DAVID MUNNS

Queen was one of the very few bands that knew how to survive.

I think Freddie always really knew what he could get away with, what the public would take. He was ahead of everybody else like that. He was just one of those fantastic guys. He loved the life. Loved the music business, lived for it. He worked at it every day. Never stopped. Enjoyed it. He'd never have stopped. His records may have become a little less frequent but he'd have never given it up. He never blamed the record company if a record wasn't a hit. He knew when a record wasn't happening. You never got any grief out of him, like it's everyone's fault but his.

EMI was a good record company for him. He got his own way with most things because he was usually always right. Jim Beach did a fantastic job for him too, he really understood that Freddie had the rightest creative instincts that anyone could have had. The videos may have been wild but the records always stood on their own. If one didn't work, get another one out. No recriminations. They got on with it. No one song was ever *so* special that he said:" That's it... I'll never do better than that!" With him, it was always onto the next.

Lots of artists never recover from a big record like *Bo Rhap*. Freddie did and just got on with the next and the next.

PETER HINCE

I never thought that he would die and even though I was aware he was ill, I never feared the worst. I thought that maybe he had a cancer or multiple sclerosis or something like that and that he would get better.

On the Sunday when the papers were full of the announcement that he had Aids, I still believed he would hang in there whilst a cure was found. I always believed he was larger than life. On the evening he died, almost around the exact time as I found out later, I was on the 'phone to Crystal, one of the other *Queen* roadies, and we were talking about sending him a cheer-up card, something that would appeal to his sense of humour. "D'you fancy going water skiing?" - Something like that? "Hurry up and get better you old bastard and stop lolling around in bed..."

Later that evening, I heard the announcement that he was dead. I went into the kitchen, got a large shot of Stolichnaya vodka, which is what he always drank and toasted him. I went to bed and went to sleep.

The next day, I was a bit numb and bought all the newspapers out of (a) curiosity and (b) also to see if they'd written the truth. A few days after the funeral I spoke to all the band, called them up and arranged to get together.

I don't think I or other people realised how popular he was. Whether a grandmother or a child, everyone seems to know a *Queen* song. Songs like *Bo Rhap* were so important; the dynamics, everything. It influenced so many people. I remember driving past Hammersmith Odeon and saw that on the marquee it read: "Freddie Mercury We Will Miss You". I was amazed at how many people called me, after he died, to ask how I was, how I was coping? So many people were concerned and affected. When someone you know vaguely dies, you obviously feel sad but it doesn't hit you that hard. When Freddie died, it was a huge chunk of my life gone. So he wasn't part of my family and I had never lived in his pocket but I didn't know who to talk to about it. It stayed with me a long time; it's still with me.

I have very mixed memories of him. There were times when I thought he was the most arrogant bastard who walked the face of the earth, and then there were times when he could be the kindest person in the world. He went into deep distress about one of his cats and then could be almost dismissive of a major news headline.

His generosity is legendary but some of it was very quirky. In Yugoslavia where it was very cold, he once bought me a woollen bobble hat and gloves. Did he think I was cold loading the trunk? After Roger and Brian had bought their roadies videos, Fred asked me if I'd like anything.

"A Porsche?" I ventured.

"Don't be silly, dear. How about an odd camera? Or a record deck. Do you play records?"

Did I play records!

I learned a lot from Freddie. I think he helped me in life to do what you believe in and to keep at it. He taught me that quality will always come through in the end.

Like the late Bill Shankly always said, "Never accept second best and don't cheat the people". In Bill's case that referred to Liverpool Football Club's supporters and in Freddie's, it was the audience because they, the fans in both cases, are the ones who pay the wages. Freddie and *Queen* were renowned for putting on the best possible shows.

When I made the decision to leave *Queen*, I told the band individually that I wanted to pursue another career and they all took it in different ways. I'm pleased to say that they were all very sorry and offered me better terms to stay on. But it wasn't a question of money, it was just that I had reached a point in my life when I wanted to do something for myself. It was very nice being in *Queen*'s reflected glory, ant it was a great trip while it lasted but I'd seen too many rock 'n' roll casualties and I'd always had a feeling that I wanted to do something more creative for myself.

Freddie was almost dismissive of my decision. I don't think he really believed it but when I did eventually leave, he kindly gave me commissions to do the photography on various of his solo projects - like *The Great Pretender* and the Montserrat Caballé album - as well as other *Queen* assignments. Though he often didn't say things, he supported me and understood what I was doing.

When things weren't going right, Freddie would always be the one to snap together - "Right!" - and off things would go again. Getting on with things, not to waste time faffing around. I learned a lot from being with *Queen* but particularly Freddie.

Last time I saw him was at the twentieth celebration party at Groucho's. Last thing he said to me that night was:

"Thanks for coming. I really appreciate it."

One very odd thing that struck me after he died was that, give or take a few days, it was two hundred years since the death of Mozart and he was a bit of a one-off too.

GARY LANGAN

I suppose, at the end, the way I look at the whole situation of Freddie is that it will be a great loss to the artistic side of life. Maybe it'll take a few years for this loss to really sink into people's minds. If I hadn't been so lucky as to have spent my early years working with such a great talent, I can't really conceive of anything since those years really replacing that great segment of my life. I can only look at him as being a major part of my life in my career. I wasn't his greatest friend. I wasn't allowed to be. That's the truth; there's no point in pretending but on the other hand nobody can remove those memories of what happened in the studio making those albums, of hearing *Bo Rhap* put together for the first time. That's a moment that's mine, nobody else's and it's because of Freddie that I'm able to have that memory and I thank him for that. It was totally unique.

What I admired at the time he was alive was the truth and the honesty that my staff at the studios showed towards Freddie. Right up until his final moments, his life and the way he wanted to live it was completely respected. That's what he inspired in people.

CHRIS TAYLOR

I knew that Freddie had Aids about a year before he died. I told no one, not even my girlfriend. Previously, though I'd been worried 'cos I knew his lifestyle, the only thing I ever knew was that he was suffering from a liver complaint. He came into the studio one day and announced that his doctor had forbade him vodka, his usual tipple. As we digested this information he added quickly:

"So get me a brandy!"

When his true condition was announced in the press, two days before he died, I got on the 'phone to my friends and said I didn't think he'd see Christmas. Lo and behold, on cue, a couple of days later and he'd snuffed it. A friend of mine rang up and told me. I watched *Sky News* to see more. I called Dave Richards in Montreux, Trip in the States and Ratty. It didn't seem to sink in.

It's not like a relative dying. There was no escape. Everyone was playing *Queen* songs all day. Trip called me from the States and told me not to get too depressed and to go and get utterly obliterated 'cos it was what Freddie would have wanted.

A couple of days later, I passed by the house to drop off a card to the guys in the house. There were all these punters outside. I never realised how big he was. I'd never seen him as this mega-rock star. I just saw him as my mate, Fred.

If I could do it all over again, I would and I guess all 'the family' would say the same. Melina's family.

BILLY SQUIER

I wrote this the day after he died. It came out pretty quickly, over the course of the afternoon; it was not a laborious process (perhaps his famous spontaneity was with me at last). When you lose someone you love, someone who is so important to you, there is a tremendous sense of futility and nothingness. I wanted so desperately to do something - for him and for myself... but what? Well, this is what I do and what he will always be to me.

I have watched you fly -
time... slipping through our fingers all the time...
you can say it doesn't matter
time... always seems the last thing on your mind...
'til one day it's all behind you

you were not the one to say that love comes cheap...
you gave your everything and more - that what you wanted

I have watched you fly... and I have shared your freedom...
can't believe my eyes - can it be it's over now...
I can't say goodbye to all those dreams we started...
'cause I have watched you fly... I want you back where you belong

Why... you could never be too careful with your life...
always reaching out for something...
life... one lonely chance to touch the stars so high...
did you risk it all for nothing?

we have some so far... but is the cost too steep?
to give up everything... everything you wanted.

I have watched you fly... and I have shared your struggle
and somewhere down inside, I know your love will keep me strong
you have lost your heart, but you have shown your courage
and I will do my part to make it right when you are gone

time... fly, fly on..............

TONY HADLEY

For me, it's the end of an era.

No one ever likes to see someone as young as Freddie dying. It's tragic. But when someone you knew and respected and thought of as friend goes...

The guy was such a talent and such a caring person. You read about so many shits in this business that when your idol turns out to be such a good egg. I just can't think.

It's just a complete tragedy.

TIM RICE

He was incredibly unpretentious, quite the opposite to what idiots might think. He was totally and utterly unpretentious. His tongue always seemed to be in his cheek. Yet, at the same time, he had the ability to say the saddest things, often in the middle of the heaviest rock context imaginable. *Hammer To Fall, We Are The Champions* are two songs that come to mid which illustrate that. He was never one to assume he was saving the world, no one can but if the world *is* to be saved, it's by Freddie's way rather than other more pompous ways.

He was ahead of his time, as far as opera was concerned, trying to bring that medium closer to his own. Opera is now very popular, the public having taken Pavaroti and the many others to their hearts. Freddie could have really taken advantage of that now. He also had an incredible set of pipes himself, very operatic. One could almost think of him as an opera singer.

As *Barcelona* is now going to be the *BBC* song for the '92 Olympics, one hopes that the Caballé album will reach a wider audience.

Having done just a little work with Freddie on two theatrical type songs on the *Barcelona* Album, *Fallen Priest* and *Golden Boy*, I do think it would have been terrific to have written something in the Offenbach vein for the theatre with him. True operatic stuff, always with that lighter element, Puccini rather than Wagner. That would have been the direction he could have taken off in and, unlike many composers, he would have been able to get up and perform the songs as well.

Above all, I'm convinced he would have continued with *Queen*. The ill-informed version of Freddie at one time in the tabloid music press wanting to portray himself as exhibitionistic and outshining the other members of *Queen* is totally wrong. The team was everything to Freddie.

ANN ORTMAN

I felt terrible about the illness and the death. The illness I sort of knew about although no one close to him ever said anything explicit. There was just a horrible, telling silence when Freddie's health was mentioned or if I enquired. The death... Well, that upset me a great deal, much more than I would have thought. I don't know why; after all, : didn't think I knew him that well.

Everyone can talk about his talent and his voice but I did love his voice.

It's just such a terrible loss; he was so young. He'd achieved the success he'd wanted, of course and I suppose that there was little in that way he could go on to do in the area he was in but that's no argument or reason for dying so young. We have too few people like that with so much to offer.

Although people say that no one is indispensable, it's not really true. He was a star and we need our stars. At least, I do. There aren't enough of them.

DIANA MOSELEY

I met Freddie at the outset of my career. Meeting him first spoiled me as I set out thinking that all other singers and bands with whom I would be working would be as inspiring and as nice as Freddie. Of course, I have worked with many nice people and many very creative people but Freddie stood apart - he was very special and very particular.

His attention to detail was phenomenal. He would take each of my working drawings for costumes and alter them, changing colour or lines himself. His eye was incredible and his ability to cross-reference into other media like opera and understand intuitively what I was trying to achieve was always so fulfilling.

When the *MAGIC* tour came into London, he saw me before the show and said:

"Tonight, I'm wearing every single costume!"

And he did. I felt so flattered. I felt he was doing it for me.

I have so much to remember. The Hat Party at which I made all the hats for him and his household. All the videos... *The Great Pretender* I remember as being especially fun to do. *I'm Going slightly Mad* was one of the last I worked on. I walked into the room and I must admit that I was shocked to see him. I hope I didn't let my concern show. He was so frail and his face looked so pained, I wondered if we were indeed going to be able to put make-up on to achieve the really brilliant effects he had envisaged. He was still fanatical about detail. He wondered if he could have hair extensions to create the right look. It was all so ironic. The song was marvellous and so apt. But he was determined and by the end of the meeting his obvious condition had been set aside and he was down on the floor again, drawing, sketching and making choices.

I couldn't believe how he put himself through all that preparation but he did. It was, after all, his job.

The very last time I saw him was at his house. He'd bought many pieces of Empire antique furniture for his homes in London and Switzerland. I'd taken some swatches of material round. He was in slippers and dressed in the cashmere dressing gown coat I'd made for him. He was still picking up furniture and rearranging it, even as weak as he was. He ordered a glass of champagne for me although he himself drank nothing and then he got tired and put his feet up onto the sofa.

I thought it was time to go and as I was leaving he said:

"Well, thank you so much for spending the afternoon with such an old man."

"No!" I said quickly, "I've just spent the afternoon with Freddie."

TREVOR CLARKE

I found the last weeks of his life very difficult. There was no question in my mind as to what was happening to him but you must understand that although I was a frequent visitor to his house, Freddie had never actually told me that he was ill. It was the same with many of those whom I would never have thought of as his very close friends.

So, there was no crack in the door, no way I felt I could comfortably, both for him and for me, go on pretending that everything was fine. After his birthday in September I never saw him again. I'd bought him some shirts, two shirts which I couldn't afford but which I knew he would love and I knew it was going to be his last birthday. However much I wanted him to miraculously rally, and survive, and live to see the Olympics in Barcelona, I knew my hopes were in vain.

Lately, I've found myself in some rather deeper financial water than I would usually have swum in, and there came a time very recently when I was faced with the bailiffs implementing an order which had been made on my flat against which I had borrowed money for a business venture. Though I'd been fighting this every which way I'd known how, I was nevertheless faced with eviction the following day and I'd decided to have a night out on the town with my last fifteen pounds of cash which would have gone no way at all to fulfil the amount I owed.

In the middle of a crowded nightclub, Jim Hutton found me. Jim, as many of you know, was Freddie's lover and he had heard of my impending eviction. He pressed a cheque into my hand and said:

"Freddie would never have had you sleep on the street."

The cheque was for the amount I needed to keep my home.

Of course, I said:

"Thank you, Jim."

Jabbing his finger skywards, Jim replied:

"Don't thank me, thank Freddie."

Not only for that but for having had the privilege of pressing your doorbell any time I wanted and needed, 'mother', thank you.

SARAH STANDING

I was living in Los Angeles when Freddie died. Of course there were rumours flying wildly about but I think I'd known for about six months or a year that he had Aids although I hadn't seen him for three or four years.

My husband John was away filming somewhere and I was alone in the house. The news of his death flashed up on the midnight bulletin and I felt an overwhelming sadness. As is the horror when famous people who are performers die, there are always films and concert clips shown portraying them as very much alive. As these were shown, it just seemed incomprehensible to me that for someone as fit and virile and standing up there on-stage, larger than life with the world at his feet could possibly be dead at such a young age, from such a dreadful disease which like a wind rips through a forest just taking people willy nilly in their prime. I just found the whole thing very very upsetting.

When you live in America for any length of time, you get so used to 'celebrities' talking publicly about their problems... Alcoholism, drug abuse, their hideous childhoods, their sexual abuse. I thought Freddie showed incredible dignity in that he didn't make or allow to have made an industry out of his having Aids. Of course, after his death the industry sprang up but at least he didn't have to see it.

I've been closer to other people who have died of Aids, including a child in Los Angeles, but somehow their deaths didn't affect me as much as his did. He was synonymous with being alive to me. His whole body, his face, everything about him was always so animated that he was almost like a cartoon, always another frame to come, always on the move.

SARAH HARRISON

Sadness; that we had lost contact during the last couple of years. Sadness; that I never actually wrote to him to say that we thought that Innuendo was the best album ever. Sadness; that someone who was once so close had taken refuge behind the walls of that fabulous house to face the knowledge of impending death surrounded by a very small nucleus of his once large circle of friends. Selfish sadness that he had cut himself off from most people to face whatever was left of the future with dignity and fortitude but without allowing most of the people who loved him to say goodbye.

Freddie had a great capacity to inspire love and affection in everyone who knew him but, at the same time, the more famous he became the less one felt that you could just ring him at the drop of a hat. Although I always had news through mutual friends, I kept putting off the dread acknowledgement that he too was going to succumb to the dreadful plague which had already taken so many friends. I know that Freddie would have faced the end with courage and strength, taking comfort from the people he was with but we who are left behind are tortured by thoughts of what might have been and of what we should have done.

Although I knew, finally, how ill he was, I had no idea that the end was so near and , since we live in France, hadn't had the current newspapers to keep us up to date.

However, although expected, the news of his death triggered off such rage in me at a life still in its prime being snuffed out and such grief that a talent which was obviously getting better and better had been lost to us.

More than that, there was the realisation that someone who had been a true friend was gone. Freddie was able to give so much because he was at ease with himself and although achieving this was no doubt personally hard, he thus had no need for pretence.

I've thought of Freddie so constantly since he died... every day without fail, in fact. His death has also seemed to have the effect of making the music of *Queen* even more popular. One can't turn on the television, enter a supermarket never mind listen to the radio without hearing those dulcet tones ringing out! I'm listening to *Bohemian Rhapsody* right now so... more power to their arm!

Fortunately, for all of us, we do have Freddie's wonderful music to remember him by and I will cherish all my own memories of a man who was a consummate showman, a good and generous friend and who loved most of all to be as outrageous as he could possibly be!

NIGEL QUINEY

A couple of weeks after I had moved house, I went to Freddie's last birthday party. His forty fifth.

Deep down I had guessed about his condition years before but I had to watch his powerful frame slowly shrink. I remember thinking when I first met him that he was developing a tum and as the same thing had happened to me, I thought how much more important it was for him to do something about it before it developed into an over thickening of the waist. The waist of course did stop thickening and there came the time when his body re-established a more youthful proportion. But it didn't stop there... That was when I knew.

There was nothing to say. I had seen it before. Other friends of mine were either in the same condition or had died. I knew from experience that the first word must come from the sufferer and that without it, one had to turn a blind eye.

The forty fifth birthday party was less attended than others. Three or four months prior, he had confided his condition and at least now, one did not have to avoid the obvious.

His spirit was extraordinary under the circumstances and he laughed and joked. He was shortly leaving for Switzerland and promised that when he got back he would like to see my new house. We made an earlier date and he came over for lunch a few days after his birthday, before going away. He was very weak and needed a helping hand but once settled on a settee enthused about the house and could obviously see its potential. I had already improved the upper floor rather dramatically and had to describe to Freddie what I had done as there was no question of him negotiating the flight of stairs.

We finally had tea and I got out part of my collection of Picturegoer weekly magazine from the forties and fifties. It was as though I had presented him with an enormous box of very fancy chocolates.

All those names... Those fabulous faces, photographed with such skill under such perfect lighting. The stories of life with the stars and of the stars at home with their perfect families. The descriptions of romantic evenings at famous Hollywood nightspots with our Hollywood Queen on the arm of a handsome escort; she, wearing tiny white gloves and staring lovingly at her beau... How we laughed! Not at them but for them, enjoying the artifice of the creation of stardom.

How ironic, I thought, that most of the stars we were looking at were dead and there was I, in my own sitting room, with one of the greatest star of the world of music, knowing that he would soon be joining them.

I never saw Freddie again.

CHERRY BROWN

I'd suspected for some time that things weren't quite right. Rumours flew back and forth and in this day and age, I'm afraid I believed them.

The sadness hit me not only when Freddie died but first, when I heard *The show Must Go On.*

Here was a song written by a man who knew he was dying, who knew that he couldn't have *that* long. And it was such a beautiful song; I think that it was what destroyed me. I can't listen to it without getting goose pimples. To think that Freddie had in fact written his feelings and set these feelings in a song... I thought it was such a wonderfully brave thing to have done. Yet I'm glad that his showmanship appeared to take him through to the end.

I hope he was surrounded by people who really cared about him and whom he wanted to have around him. It seems to be so easy when you're a superstar to become surrounded by people whom you wouldn't really have chosen; people who have just appeared.

ELAINE PAIGE

Freddie was a complete original; individual, vulnerable, kind and always sensitive to others. As an artist, his contribution to music has been phenomenal. As a friend, one always felt that time spent with him had been valuable, relaxed and very rewarding. We all benefited from his enthusiasm for life which was so inspiring.

JAMES ARTHURS

"I think for each of the fifteen years I knew Freddie we got together every Christmas except two, when we were in different countries. We'd meet usually on Christmas Eve, nights which ended up with drunken but happy carolling sessions, always exaggerated of course and sometimes with Freddie on piano. We did our separate things on Christmas day and then there was always a party once again on Boxing Day, mostly at his place, which went on until dawn broke. I don't know how we found the energy then but the talk and the laughs just went on and on and on until we'd either drop exhausted or go our separate ways.

That was the first thing I felt when I came to London at Christmas in 1991. There was a void.

Something wasn't the same. That Christmas, only a few weeks after his death, was the first time it struck me that Freddie really wasn't there any longer and I couldn't believe it.

I called on Mary Austin and went out with Straker and spent my usual Christmas day with my family but despite the fun and merriment, there was always this vague, gnawing, empty feeling. I remembered the previous Christmas when Freddie and I had sat alone for a couple of hours, just chatting while everyone else had gone out. Freddie was virtually lecturing me to look after myself and to avoid the excesses. "We're too old for all that shit any more, dear and it's boring when you've done it all." We hugged and kissed goodbye a few hours later and now I only have memories.

Good memories. Fun memories, lifted up into that caravan of extravagance and carried along with never-ending laughs through all the excesses. I'll miss him forever but he'll always be there for the good things never go away."

PETER FREESTONE

He was the most kind and generous man I ever met. He taught me so much about so many things. Art ... appreciation, creating, creativity ... Even patience although he himself was always so impatient. As far as I'm concerned, Freddie was the teacher and when he died, school was out forever and it was then up to us to go out and make use of what we'd learned, what he'd taught us.

He was that rare being, a man who had impeccable taste and yet also the wherewithal to effect that taste. He was in private life exactly as he was when working in the studio. He didn't care how much anything cost in terms of money or time or effort provided that the end result was as perfect as the idea he had first had in his mind.

Quite simply, he got things done and those things were always done the way he wanted them done.

EPILOGUE

August 1995

FOUR YEARS ON ...

Four years on, I feel very differently. Four years on, I don't think I could write *This is the Real Life...* My feelings about all our real lives, both present and past, are four years older. Four years ... wiser? Probably not. The individual sets of truths contained in *This is the Real Life..* do not seem in any way to have been invalidated by this passing of time but, perforce, they have been exposed to hindsight and hindsight, like explosive, if used whimsically and emotively can be a very dangerous commodity. Hindsight can commute kindly hope into frustrating disappointment, fond memory into itching irritation. Sorry Mr. Keats, but distance does not always lend enchantment to the view ... Not for everyone. It's a little like the *Qué Sera* song ... What will be, will be. Fine for some; but for everyone?

Four years on, it seems in many ways that Freddie's Real Life is breaking up both as a reality and as a memory faster than most. What has happened in the aftermath of Freddie's death is what happens in so many cases of gay bereavement. The family and/or the powers-that-be re-absorb and cleanse their black sheep who re-emerge from the dipping as fluffy, whitened, designer baa-lambs. The deceased's home is sold or re-inhabited, the partner is edged out, collections of possessions dispersed, friends drift away ... Seldom is there a focus left for The Real Life to be celebrated in any way other than over time and distance by separated people and the inevitable happens ...

The once-clear image begins to break up as we all get on with our lives and go our separate ways, never to reassemble as little pieces of the whole truth. Colours fade, sounds echo then disappear. That wonderful singing yellow of the Garden Lodge dining room, the yellow of turmeric and saffron and the spice and zing of a Zanzibar street market now glows less brightly in my mind's eye; the Rudi Patterson paintings on the wall seem less distinct, bleached by time of their vibrant, tropic colour. That thrilling sound of clinking glasses, champagne-filled or wine-brimming which used to trill like a carillon of tiny Indian ankle bells throughout the ground floor ... How did the old Jacobite toast go? "To the King Across the Water!" Water or whatever. Time or tide. Death or exile ... They're gone.

As far as Freddie's aftermath is concerned, the statue of our boy which was so much publicised seems as far away from installation as ever. It seems that no location can be agreed upon or properly granted although I have been assured that there is a sculptor's model from which casts have been made. Kenny Everett, a very important influence on Freddie in the early days and a friend (bar the latter-day shouting), sadly died earlier this year. Straker and I went to his services at the Mount Street Catholic Church and remembered a day far far away in 1979 when Freddie, Joe, Straker, Me, Kenny and John Pitt went out for lunch and then were given a mystery tour. The destination was Garden Lodge, newly bought and un-converted. Freddie was so thrilled. It was a lovely, bright sunny day and the garden shrubs, including camellia bushes, were in full bloom. Kenny had just acquired one of the lately introduced video cameras and shot mad zany footage of us, acting out a silly take-off of Greta Garbo playing the dying Margaret Gautier in 'La Dame aux Camellias'. Never had one garden seen so much dying. Or, so we might have been forgiven then for thinking. Now, as I write, only half of our number that happy afternoon are still, to my knowledge, alive. We are indeed a shrinking band of witnesses.

Another marker has been the exhibition of Freddie's stamp collection ... Although, like with most of us and the popular boys' hobby of stamps, Freddie stopped collecting when he was very young, his stamps have been seen now in many places and the fan club convention in Southport was regaled by Derrick Page of London's National Postal Museum who explained the philatelic significance of the collection.

And then, of course, there has been *Mercury and Me*, Jim Hutton's book. When reading Jim's book - which I hope you do for there is much of great value and heartfelt sincerity within it - please don't read it like you were reading about an 'ordinary' couple. They weren't and if you do, you'll be insulting your own intelligence as well as the relationship the two men had. Man and wife the books says ... No, Jim. I really like you and respect you enormously but as a gay man, writing (putatively) in the mid-nineteen nineties, *surely* you don't mean that?

As innocently as the work was undertaken, I fear that it was so written by Tim Wapshott, the actual writer of the book, as to make what was a difficult, nay impossible, domestic situation often sound like a scene from Snow White. The evil queen blows hot and cold and does a lot of huff and puff acting whilst the courtiers struggle petulantly for attention, the consort an oft-marginalised figure. Wapshott's journalistic style unfortunately rendered the reality of a situation which must have been very hard both for him and for many of the book's targeted readers to comprehend into a cartoon, a form which, admittedly, could at least be easily digested.

Jim and Freddie's domestic situation was infinitely more complicated than Wapshott was able to explain. Garden Lodge was not only a home; it was more akin to the court of a potentate. There were staff, work men and women and functionaries as well as the residents who themselves were also employees. And what of the love, do I hear you ask? Love is, as they sang in *The Desert Song*, where you find it and that it was found at all in the latter years at Garden Lodge is a real triumph of romance over circumstances, or, at least a prolonged suspension of disbelief.

Garden Lodge wasn't a fairyland castle. It was an essential and necessary court. It developed empirically for very good reasons. Freddie needed the household which he allowed to arrive in order for him to prosper further when he was well and, even more importantly, survive as long as possible when he was ill. It was The Real Life which threw up the candidates for the positions in the household. They weren't sought nor were the vacancies ever advertised for. The tide of living washed yet more of The Real life in. Freddie's was a totally organic life in that respect and living it was never smooth. Like Jim Hutton's stories of doors opening and then doors slamming, Joe Fanelli too came and went so many times, people lost count. After his love relationship with Freddie broke up, he lived away for some years before returning to the household in an employed position. Freddie could not afford to have what had flowed in ebb away regarding loyalty and trustworthiness. The Real Life, with perhaps one exception, furnished him, truly, fortunately.

The one possible exception was, of course, Paul Prenter who is dead and whose confidences are thus restricted to newspaper coverage, for which and over which he was equally hounded. Prenter's Queenobilia has also been sold off by him and his estate at various sales and whatever price they fetched was entirely relevant for Paul Prenter was an intimate and fully accredited member of the inner circle of The Real Life for the years when Freddie had no permanent partner during those party-party years. Paul Prenter's ghost looms large over the smoking battlements, like Banquo's. In 1977, Prenter had been employed to work with all four members of *Queen* first via John Reid, with whom his history stretched back to Tamla Motown days, although when the management move away from Reid and to Beach took place, Prenter moved too. Later on, his affinity with Freddie was validated by their mutual interests and proclivities and when Freddie's life veered off in the dual directions of Munich and New York, Paul Prenter was a prime mover and shaker in Fred's increasingly extravagant lifestyle.

As far as other markers, I understand there have been other books but I haven't read them. That sounds caddish and it's not meant. It's just that recently I read a volume about Ibiza and found the writer irresponsibly stating that Freddie spent his last summer in Roger Taylor's house on the island. The writer might just have easily said that Fred spent the summer in aisle three in Sainsbury's on the Cromwell Road.

Before logging some other observations and recording other events, there is, however, one thing which has marked the boy's passing in a sensible and positive (ugh! that word!) way and that is the Mercury Phoenix Trust.

I have just spoken with Ann Meyer at Festival Services in Montreux in Switzerland where Jim Beach, *Queen*'s manager, has based the business operation which looks after *Queen*'s interests and, presumably, those affairs of the individual band members which are not dealt with on a day-to-day basis in Great Britain.

I wanted to find out more about the Mercury Phoenix Trust and Jim Beach, whilst reserving his and the members of *Queen*'s right not to talk about Freddie in the body of this book, had given his permission for Ann to speak to me about the Mercury Phoenix Trust.

It was set up in 1992 to deal with the income derived from the Tribute Concert, ticket sales, broadcasting income, recording royalties et cetera. The trustees are Jim Beach, Brian May, Roger Taylor and Mary Austin ... John Deacon is not a trustee, declining presumably for the same reasons which another rumour has it almost compelled him not to participate in the Tribute Concert itself. The MPT is registered as a charity at The Charity Commission, Number 1013768 and in the year April 1992 - March 1993, the only year for which it has registered accounts at the time of writing, had an income of some £1,400,000. The royalty proceeds from the Christmas sales of *Bohemian Rhapsody* in 1991/92 - well over a million pounds so Ann tells me - had already been donated directly to the Terence Higgins Trust prior to the Mercury Phoenix Trust's inception and the income derived in the USA from the Fox TV Broadcasts (ironically a Rupert Murdoch-owned network) and the re-released *Bohemian Rhapsody* USA royalties were distributed directly to AIDS charities across the States.

The Trust received further income from royalties derived from the George Michael *Five Live* mini-album and of course there have been the continuing contributions which extraordinary members of the public have made to the MPT via Maureen Barclay and her band of two hundred devoted volunteers who collect annually, the week in particular including that period between the anniversary of Freddie's death and World Aids Day on December 1st.

The trustees adjudicate the distribution of funds on the basis of applications sent in from all over the world and in particular where they feel that the work of the supplicant projects and institutions is not one which is being funded by the governments of the relevant countries. Applications have been received and funds distributed to African projects, Indian, Thai and some in Mexico as well as many U.K. based projects. South American requirements tend to be covered by the major UK-based fund-raising organisations such as Crusaid and Terence Higgins Trust which the Mercury Phoenix Trust has helped.

The types of project which MPT funds are front line organisations dealing with hospice care, preventative care and support groups and the funds tend to be core funds, i.e. providing a pivot around which further funds are collected by the organisation either from other charitable sources or from private donation and collection. There are a couple of research projects, one in Holland housed in The Freddie Mercury Building which deals with genetic research in the gene architecture of those humans and monkeys who seem not to develop HIV or Aids after exposure. The second research project is based in the U.K.

Ann kindly posted me a triple fold A4 information sheet which covers fund distribution until September 1994 and indeed lists eighty eight organisations world wide which have benefited from the £1.5 million which had by then been distributed. We look forward to seeing the other two years' accounts of the Fund's work. Ann tells me that she is given to believe that the work of the Trust will be ongoing, that it will not be terminated just because no more royalty based funds devolve upon it. This is indeed good news for all those fund-raisers who have worked so hard already. It is so much easier to elicit donations when their collection is hung upon the peg of a greatly celebrated name like Freddie's. If anyone would like to join Maureen Barclay's team, please write to her at 13, The Furlongs, Needingworth, St. Ives, Cambridge-shire PE17 3TX.

I have just returned from visiting Somerset House in the Strand in London where I had seen a copy of Freddie's will, rather his final will, dated September 17th 1991, for we don't know how many others he made during the course of his long and complicated business life.

Yes, wills are business, believe me.

The implications to an organisation such as *Queen*'s for an integral party to die intestate or with a contestable will is unthinkable. The wording of Freddie's will had to obviate any confusion for both the people Freddie wished to inherit his estate and for the members of *Queen* themselves and *Queen* as an institution to go on un-encumbered by in-fighting and hassle. Freddie was very, very loyal to 'his boys'.

By nominating and totally empowering Henry James (Jim) Beach and John Libson (*Queen*'s lawyer/manager and Freddie's accountant respectively) as trustees and executors, Freddie ensured that the organisational future of *Queen* and its interests as well as the execution of his will would not be threatened by the decisions of non-Queen team members. Outsiders.

If he was, as I always saw him, the one outsider in *Queen*, Freddie in death was finally re-assimilated into the body politic of the Queen organisation, the 'mother ship' as it is gently described in the Mercury Phoenix Trust's pamphlet. No more loose cannons. All the visiting inter-planetary aliens were back on board.

The two executor/trustees were granted complete discretion in arranging for the disposal and/or distribution of Freddie's estate. Other than his shares in the various private companies in which he was involved, his will nominated his estate as including Garden Lodge, the adjoining Mews, his controlling shares in his New York apartment, 43E, at 425 East 58th Street, the contents of all these places and all his possessions. Fred empowered the Trustees to move money or similar securities wherever in the world and to be responsible for the payments to the legatees of their bequests and the implementation of the terms of the will.

Discretion is very important. Without it, it would have been difficult for the Trustees to navigate the emotionally choppy waters which would inevitably surround the death of such a wealthy unmarried man with living family. Discretion was, for example, obviously exercised in arranging for Mary, potentially the largest and, arguably, the ultimate beneficiary, to take up residence in the house in Logan Place which she presumably chose to do as per the wording of her legacy rather than liquidate her bequest by selling the house. Without this 'discretion', it could have been thorny and potentially disrupting to have to have seen The Real Life go on for any longer than respectably necessary. After what was deemed a decent period of mourning, the gay household was systematically disbanded. The King is Dead - The Court must die too.

The gross value of the assets in Freddie's estate was deemed by the Probate Court in Oxford to be worth £8,649,940. This valuation, prior to any payments even to debtors or The Inland Revenue, caused some surprise when it was made known as many people had thought Freddie to have been much wealthier, giving the lie to those specious tables of 'Britain's Wealthiest People' occasionally published in newspapers who ought really to be more responsible. The estate, (excluding the nominated shareholdings Freddie had in private companies which were passed to the care of the Trustees for administration) after accounting for debts and monies owed for example in tax, would of course have been subject to the forty percent rate of inheritance tax after the deduction of the usual individual's allowances. The net residue of Freddie's estate, i.e. including publishing and recording royalties represented by the income accruing from his shareholdings in the unspecified private limited companies, for a foreseen period chosen to last for fifty years after Fred's death until a date known as 'the vesting Day', was granted proportionately. Fifty percent was to be awarded to Mary Austin, twenty five percent each to Freddie's sister Cash Cooke and to his parents Bomi and Jer Bulsara. In the case of any of Freddie's family predeceasing her, Mary was to be the ultimate beneficiary. However, after the vesting day should even Mary no longer be living, the ultimate beneficiary of Freddie's last will and testament is not Mary Austin. The ultimate beneficiaries are The Imperial Cancer Research Fund and the National Society for Mentally Handicapped Children. There is no mention of any Aids related foundations. Freddie was not un-generous to Aids causes. I know of one small fund-raising event, a small tea party where bits and pieces were sold off to benefit Crusaid. Freddie sent a cheque for £250, a proportionately huge percentage of the £1500 afternoon's take.

A word about the gross amount of the estate for there were the usual reports of fighting and bitterness and pique surrounding the legacies. The amount confirms what I confess that I initially thought were Freddie's merely fanciful fears which he confided to me about his cash-flow. Private medical care on the scale on which it was being made available to Freddie from the Westminster Hospital is *very* expensive. Fred's outgoings in the last couple of years of his life must have been huge. Please bear in mind that the gross estate included the probate approved valuation of the New York Apartment, Garden Lodge and the Mews *and* the houses' contents *and* Fred's personal possessions as well as any cash he had in U.K. banks. A *very* large percentage of that eight and a half million *must* have been in non-liquid assets. It accounts for the rumours which reached me that Mary was finding it tough when she first moved into Garden Lodge. After duty and after the distribution of the post-Probate approved amounts of tax-free legacies £500,000 each to Jim, Joe and Peter Freestone and Terry Giddings' £100,000, there cannot have been very much cash at all.

No wonder Fred was worried ... You cannot, after all, however much of a perfectionist, be expected to time your death to the nearest convenient pound.

The residents of Garden Lodge, it is said, having been persuaded to move out, must also have been in some consternation for the months which elapsed until the will had been proved at Probate Court in Oxford in the middle of May for until then, no monies would have been forthcoming from their legacies. Ways and means would have been very unclear.

I must say I found it strange that there were no other legatees. Little somethings. Tokens. It seemed that it wasn't like the Freddie we had known over the years who had always adored the giving of gifts as much as he had loved receiving them. I rather felt he had until those last months wanted his friends and those to whom he had been close to have specific things to remember him by. He was very generous to Tony King who acted as close confidante for a period during Freddie's last months and I too know that Fred had wanted to buy me - who was not in the innermost circle of The Real Life - some thing. I think mine's a rather nice story.

About six months before he died, the telephone rang ... Could I come to lunch and we'd go to Pontevecchio in Brompton Road opposite our much-loved Coleherne pub? Yes I'd love to come ... Just lunch or anything special? ... Nothing special, dear but we'll go shopping afterwards ... Right.

Nice lunch. Just us and Terry. The shopping was a trip down the Kings Road to the premises called Rupert Cavendish, a business which sold genuine and faux Biedermeyer furniture. Apparently Elton had just been in so I rather gathered where Freddie had gotten the tip about the shop ... He was looking, he announced, at desks and what did I think? ... Where are you going to put it, dear? ... Oh, it's not for me, darling . It's for you! ... For me?

He looked at me with such a heartfelt mixture of pleading and sort of little boy who really wants to please ... It was sweet of him. On sore reflection, of course, I should have accepted a desk, any desk but at that moment they really didn't 'speak' to me and I knew that I had to make sure that my partner Nigel liked it because we always choose house things together.

This I explained. Everything? Fred replied incredulously, a vague horror underpinning the woundedness. 'Fraid so, quoth I.

And there the matter rested ... Now, of course, I can never forget the gesture for he was ratifying me as a writer. Writers write at desks, don't they?

When Fred finally came to our new house, he looked round and very quickly said, "Quite right about the desk, dear." I, of course, have written in front of many pieces of furniture but never, ever at a desk.

So ... For the survivors, lives go on. For a while, at least.

Then, first, Joe Fanelli died in America. I'd first met Joe in, I believe, 1979 when he had appeared at Stafford Terrace after having met Freddie in America. He was quite plump in those days, quite like how Freddie liked his chaps then and he seemed so very, very young and quite bemused. He was very enthusiastic and Freddie was delighted that he had found a 'husband' who was such a good cook. But Joe always, always had other talents. In the early days, he wanted to write and showed me a play of his - I believe it had something to do with elephants and elephant jokes - which betrayed at least the ability to create a full length work. In genre it was absurd and I must say I enjoyed reading it. But nothing happened to it and there were no more plays, none that I read anyway. Later, when he returned as employee to the household, Joe became a computer expert and took many classes and courses. He always displayed an inner drive to somehow better himself, to prove himself not 'just a cook'. I hope he spent every penny of his half million pounds and died at least somewhat fulfilled although his was to prove an unfulfillable destiny.

Joe's was also another admission to me about his state of health. The first occasion we sat down to discuss and map out the 'Entertaining Mr. Mercury' cookbook, Joe told me that it was only right that I should know that he was sick too ... Presumably he was inferring that he did not know how long he himself would be around to be part of the project. That was the day I realised that all was terribly wrong at Garden Lodge. His diplomatic request not to comment when I asked about Jim Hutton's health left me no alternative but to realise that there were three sick people in that household. Three sets of worries, fears, illness, uncertainty ... That there was any cheerfulness at all, ever, was nothing short of miraculous although the tensions erupted volcanically many times. That all life as we know it wasn't buried like Pompeii under a layer of white hot fallout is noteworthy.

One of the eruptions was, however, a lunch scheduled by Fred during the last visit to the U.K. of his friends Thor and Lee from San Diego. These two gentle giants, friends of Fred's from way back New

York partying days, together with Mary and myself were due to sample Joe's famous paella which had nothing to do with basic Catalan cuisine but everything to do with lobsters; although I don't think any self-respecting lobster would wish to be seen within a mile of so peasant a demise, the lobsters Joe had selected had no choice. Live they arrived at Garden Lodge, their pincers bound in thick elastic bands, never to leave. To confirm Jim's 'Death of a Koi Carp' story, Freddie hated seeing or, worse, hearing these poor screaming crustaceans die. Joe had other ideas. Oh, bear in mind it was a baking, boiling hot day, not really the moment for a Masterchef 1991 exhibition cook-out.

Whilst Freddie was in the kitchen, Joe started dropping our lunch into the huge vats of boiling water. Hearing the lobsters' dying screams, Freddie went berserk and fled in great distress to his room whilst Joe in a fury hurled the half cooked beasts around the kitchen. At times, they must have really loathed each other. All so, so tragically understandable.

When I arrived that day, I looked up to Freddie's bedroom window from outside the front door and there saw a very worried, tearful little face. His thin hand waved, bleakly.

Terry Giddings let me in very glumly. The answer to my question, "What's happened?" was only too obvious as he showed me into the kitchen. Lobster was spattered everywhere, green bits as well as pink, and Joe's ass was seen fleeing in heat and temper up the back stairs. Terry and I just looked at each other, sighed and set to with cloths to clean up.

The lunch went ahead but I can never look a proper paella in the face again and as for lobster ...

I can't begin to imagine what it must have like for those boys living in that house. Talk about gilded cages.

Peter Freestone (Phoebe) has taken up nursing. He must have learned more than enough about the caring art whilst at Garden Lodge and I'm glad that his patience and enduring good nature even under the most acrimonious barrage of Fred being really quite horrid on occasion is, therefore, now available to the public at large via the National Health Service.

Jim Hutton is doing OK. Whenever you hear anyone knocking the National Health Service, think ... Yeah, maybe ... and listen. But think also of Jim and the thousands like him who are cared for and nursed when necessary and supplied with every sort of drug and piece of equipment without the slightest let or hindrance. The really sick ones are never let down. In New York even and certainly in baseline clinics in the third world, people stand on line for hours, days sometimes, for the slightest crumb of charity when they are in dire distress and in dreadful need of care. These are the people The Mercury Phoenix Trust helps.

As for the band, Roger released another album, I recall and as far as Brian May's career is concerned, it really took off in the vacuum left by Freddie's death. The clogged one, as he is referred to in some elevated circles, has done for Ford of Dagenham what it's native offspring Sandie Shaw was never able to do in bare feet. I somehow doubt whether Freddie would have been so generous towards the giant industrial multinational. True to the spirit of Ford's generosity as expressed in his song, Brian is doing everything he does lately to provide us with another *Queen* album, featuring, so we intuit, some of Fred's more bankable unfinished warbles from the Swiss studio vaults. Of John Deacon, I have been told nothing.

Rumours abound that the Fred-less *Queen* are to tour to promote this new album and that the utterly uncontroversial George Michael is to provide the vocal focus. Another rumour is that Jim Beach has been introduced to someone who can sing so like Freddie that a theatre show is being commissioned from an eminent writer, built round this stooge performer. Sounds not unlike a *Stars In Their Eyes* situation. Meanwhile I would like it known that Peter Straker who could sing the plating off Gabriel's horn from the other side of heaven is still taking calls.

The hiccough in their friendship during the last year of Freddie's life was one of the saddest things I have ever seen two friends go through. When they first met, in 1975, theirs became the friendship of real peers. They were alike in almost every respect, vocal talent, performing technique and they were both outsiders ... Both had come to this country from other parts of the commonwealth and both were thus in their way more British than the British. Both charming, both 'gentlemen' as their schooling and upbringing had taught them to be, both, in a way, still boys. But Peter knew so much more about the world, was so much more socially adept and fielded a huge number of celebrated show-business contacts. Freddie was hugely impressed and, for a while, became the pupil. Peter rounded off a lot of Freddie's edges, showed him a style which Freddie copied and which empowered him.

Then, the tables were, of course, turned as Dame Fortune took a hand.

"I suppose you've seen him?" Freddie would ask me sharply. "You know I have," I would reply, firmly but open-endedly. But that would be that. Dame Fortune never squared the circle. There is so much unfinished business. That's the other thing death teaches.

And, as far as other as yet unfinished business is concerned, I'm pleased to report that Mike Smith has acquired an option on the rights to Jim Hutton's book *Mercury and Me* to be turned into a mini-series for TV. Who do you think will play Straker or Elaine Page or Dave Clark himself, for that matter? And Montserrat, La Superba? I wonder who will be the casting director?

David Minns, my co-author, has, over the past couple of years, sold

187

a lot of his Freddie-obilia both in Bonham's Saleroom and - despite initially being told by the *Queen* Press Office that he was bringing the reputation of the band into disrepute by offering his items for sale - to Jim Beach who is now the proud owner of some of Freddie's own painting. Mercury Songs were the lucky buyer but one ponders with a puzzled frown the irony of Freddie's company buying back his artwork. Was it really to protect a reputation which didn't need protecting at all because everyone knew? David Minns assures me that all the artwork, suitably scanned and reproduced, would make an admirable set of greetings cards if sold via the Mercury Phoenix Trust. Just an idea, of course. It would be nice. David is now thankfully recovered from a serious heart attack and resulting quintuple bypass heart surgery.

Which leaves Mary.

Almost at the beginning of my friendship with Freddie, I felt deeply for Mary who I knew was going to be hurt as a result of Freddie's coming out. As long as he remained bisexual, Mary still had a place in Freddie's life. To my way of thinking, as soon as he declared his colours, flew them from his mast and lived by their tenets, I knew Mary would be marginalised, probably left behind. Had I been Mary, I wouldn't have waited. I wasn't Mary, thank heavens, for what she did and continued to do for sixteen years was to persistently hang in.

It was pointed out very early on to Freddie that Mary, had she so desired, could have made a good case in law when he 'left' her - for make no mistake, leave her is exactly what he did - that she was his common-law wife and as such entitled to a share of his wealth. And quite right is what I thought at the time. She and her earnings had helped support him whilst he was becoming Freddie Mercury and she had every right to reap the fair, proportionate rewards of the success Freddie Mercury became.

Friends they must indeed have been for her good fortune to have been so provided for in his will but as far as anything else is concerned ... Does it matter? That they were friends is all that needs to be said about their relationship. What's wrong with being friends? Millions of married people aren't. What's so great about being someone's wife or 'girlfriend' if you're not their friend? What's so great about married, about sex? Freddie, for whatever reasons - probably a cocktail of caveats, courtesy and caring - indeed allowed Mary to want for nothing, including her in all the house parties The Real Life engendered, providing a nominal job in his household and buying a flat for her to live in. In that way, the intervening years passed.

Mary is a particular, private woman. As a very young woman, as an ex-Biba girl, she had a wide-eyed, etiolated sixties beauty which was remote and which seemed almost vapid. It seemed you could draw anything on her face, create any personality. Mary's parents were both deaf and dumb and her growing up was done in a situation where she was in charge, communicating for them. She always seemed anxious, serious and when seen with the other *Queen* ladies who all dressed a great deal in black at the time, contributed to the feeling that they were like the chorus of Trojan women, about to intone some doleful litany of woe and disaster.

But then, I suppose, Mary had had little to be cheerful about. She had grown-up as her parents' mouthpiece in their silent world. It must have been a huge burden to have carried and it produced a quiet, introverted, masked personality who smiled only occasionally. And she cannot, surely, have been immune to wondering exactly what Mr. Bulsara-turned-Mercury was doing out 'til all hours? 'The Studio, darling' is not ultimately a convincing panacea chitty. It's not unlike the 'Forgot my kit, sir' blanket excuse which some of us used at school to get out of the games or physical education we loathed.

Mary, usually, seemed nervous and uncomfortable and yet, one-on-one, could talk in torrents on the telephone for hours and hours about her situation with Freddie, or her boyfriend Joe, or her flat or whatever ... She always had my sympathy and always had my ear available.

Mary is patently far from vapid. That she hung on in a situation from which most women would have bowed out to find a heterosexual milieu more suited to the needs of independent life is indeed a feat both of perseverance and, it has to be said, acting for I honestly believe that she never was at ease in the gay company with which Freddie surrounded himself. I could sense her unease and, as far as I could, compensated for it, consciously toning down some of my own behaviour to accommodate her essentially heterosexual femininity. Mary was never 'one of the boys' as so many of the women were in Freddie's life. She appeared not to have that glorious, ebullient self-confidence of a Barbara Valentin or Anna Nicholas or Anita Dobson or Diana Mosley ... All wonderfully talented and strong women who were not threatened by Freddie's outrageousness one bit. In fact, they were validated by it.

Mary was always remote, removed in spirit and in flesh from The Real Life. That she remained part of The Real Life is however undeniable. Make of it what you will but it actually puzzled and saddened me. Like his parents, like many families - and there is no reason why they inherently should or even can - I feel that Mary never understood gay life and gay lives and in my opinion condoned neither.

What gladdened me, therefore, was Piers Cameron's arrival on the scene - entirely approved of by Freddie - and Mary's resulting pregnancy which produced their son, Richard. I really thought that with Piers, Mary had achieved a relationship which could allow her at long last to remove herself from what I always considered the unhealthy clinging on to a situation which could only ever compound the initial grief and heart-break from which it is obvious that she had never recovered.

However, Mary's and Piers' future as committed partners was not to be and as has been widely reported, they are now separated.

Freddie, sad to report, treated Mary's coming legacy rather too cavalierly. At a lunch at Garden Lodge not two weeks after Mary told me that she and Piers were to separate, Freddie flashed a saleroom catalogue in my face and pointed to a huge diamond-encrusted feather brooch and, with Mary sitting between us at the table, told me: "I've told her to bid whatever she needs to for it ... After all, she's going to get it all when I've gone!"

He was a naughty boy sometimes. I don't know if Jim was at lunch - probably not - but what a perspective, I thought, for him to have lived with in a house that was rapidly turning into a burial chamber, stuffed full, like a latter day Tutankhamun's, of goodies that *this* pharaoh knew he couldn't take with him.

I'm sure the train of events which Jim Hutton has chronicled in his book leading up to the boys' departure from Garden Lodge and Mary's arrival is entirely accurate. She was always irritated at never having been bought a house but merely being, as it were, a grace and favour tenant of a company-owned apartment, however commodious. What happened, therefore, happened. I know Freddie didn't *want* it to happen but I reckon he knew there was nothing he could do to prevent the 'deluge' which ensued 'aprés moi', any comparison between our boy and France's Sun King and his fabled Versailles being entirely coincidental, of course! More seriously, I would have obviously thought it would have been more sympathetic to have allowed the Garden Lodge residents to remain at least until the financial provision of the will had been sorted out but, as Freddie would have said himself, "Well, dears, there you have it."

Qué sera, indeed.

So there we have it. Mary now lives in Garden Lodge and the Mews as a single parent family, raising the two little Cameron children, Richard and his younger brother James who missed Freddie by about a couple of months as he wasn't born until 1992. They live in what I can only imagine - having not been back there - is a cross between a mausoleum and a fortress and indeed Mary has just had the height of the fencing atop the garden wall increased. I hope the 'fabulador des quimeras' - the myth-and-monster maker that Mr. Mercury could occasionally, inadvertently of course, be - hasn't created a labyrinth and housed in it a latter-day minotaur.

I always remember Jim Beach's wife Claudia saying at one of Freddie's parties that "... we owe everything we have to Freddie." If Freddie's aftermath has any meaning, it really is just that. Acknowledgement of debt. Everyone, I contend, who came into contact with Freddie ended up owing him. For his friends and family involved in The Real Life, he provided and gave so much more than he ever borrowed, stole or requisitioned. Everyone, that is, except one very, very important person.

The fans. For Freddie, in his turn, owed everything he had to the fans.

Personally, writing this book taught me never, ever to ridicule or take lightly or for granted the fans. I knew Freddie was loved. I always knew that. I had absolutely no idea how incredibly important his and *Queen*'s lives and careers are to thousands and thousands of people throughout the world. Bearing that observation in mind, Claudia Beech's remark didn't go far enough. What she might have said is that, "... we owe everything we have to Freddie's fans." That's the bottom line. Without the fans, the punters, there would have never been a Freddie Mercury and no one would have owed anyone anything.

Through the writing of this book, I have been introduced to Margaret Gorman and Ann Christe. Just two fans, you might suppose ... But no. Two women in my own age group, quite un-hysterical, centred, calm with families and grown children of their own. The questions they ask, what they want to know is nothing smutty, or salacious but erstwhile, earnest and life-affirming. These women and all the hundreds and thousands of people like them have spent a great deal of money as well as time on Freddie and Queen and they have derived an intense and vital pleasure from listening to Freddie, the band and that wonderful repertoire of songs. I can but acknowledge their interest and respect. Once my initial cynicism to their enquiries had been stiffed, they helped me to revise my learning of a basic lesson: life is never a clean slate. For everything I owe you, you owe to someone else and so on ad infinitum. It is an endless cycle of acknowledgement.

The Fred 'n' *Queen* publicity machine grinds on and it will do so as long as there is money to be made from *Queen* and its derivatives. To make publicity work, the flow of information has to be controlled. If there were no secrets, there would be no surprises and the news desks wouldn't perk up at the arrival of an *Official Queen* or Freddie press release. So, I can never answer all those questions that Margaret and Ann would love to have answered because The Real Life will never be reassembled.

Maybe Freddie's parents and family really don't want to know anything about what they used to call 'that other business' - The Real Life. All I can muster, if that is indeed the situation, is that I know of several families who have benefited hugely after their children's deaths from meeting their children's friends and loved ones with whom they would probably never have otherwise come in contact. We are all only what we truly are through the acknowledgement of those whom we know and love and who, in turn, know and love us.

Maybe the official *Queen* establishment have no need or no time or no inclination to acknowledge that the unofficial friends and fans are also part of the greater picture, the truer truth. Any degree of the truth is neither good nor bad, harmful nor capricious. It is merely truth. What other people, what *we* do with it is, however, is quite 'another business'.

Although I am told we are judged by the company we keep, what we are of any lasting value at all can only be seen by and reflected in the eyes of our company of friends, associates and family, anyone who thinks fondly of us. It seems that it is only when we no longer exist that the real 'us' can be accounted for. When else except after a death would *all* that company gather in one place to pay their respects. This book still stands as one such place for Freddie. But, like his funeral, there was room at the end of The Real Life for so many, many more.

Freddie Mercury died on November 24th, 1991
but the legacy of his music will live with us forever.